A publication of

The National Association
for Sport and Physical Education

an association of

American Alliance
for Health, Physical Education,
Recreation and Dance

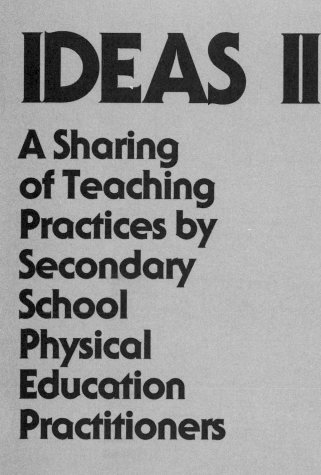

IDEAS II

A Sharing of Teaching Practices by Secondary School Physical Education Practitioners

Edited by
Ronald P. Carlson

Copyright © 1984

American Alliance for
Health, Physical Education,
Recreation and Dance

1900 Association Drive
Reston, Virginia 22091

ISBN 0-88314-264-3

Purposes of the American Alliance For Health, Physical Education, Recreation and Dance

The American Alliance is an educational organization, structured for the purposes of supporting, encouraging, and providing assistance to member groups and their personnel throughout the nation as they seek to initiate, develop, and conduct programs in health, leisure, and movement-related activities for the enrichment of human life.

Alliance objectives include:

1. Professional growth and development—to support, encourage, and provide guidance in the development and conduct of programs in health, leisure, and movement-related activities which are based on the needs, interests, and inherent capacities of the individual in today's society.

2. Communication—to facilitate public and professional understanding and appreciation of the importance and value of health, leisure, and movement-related activities as they contribute toward human well-being.

3. Research—to encourage and facilitate research which will enrich the depth and scope of health, leisure, and movement-related activities; and to disseminate the findings to the profession and other interested and concerned publics.

4. Standards and guidelines—to further the continuous development and evaluation of standards within the profession for personnel and programs in health, leisure, and movement-related activities.

5. Public affairs—to coordinate and administer a planned program of professional, public, and governmental relations that will improve education in areas of health, leisure, and movement-related activities.

6. To conduct such other activities as shall be approved by the Board of Governors and the Alliance Assembly, provided that the Alliance shall not engage in any activity which would be inconsistent with the status of an educational and charitable organization as defined in Section 501(c) (3) of the Internal Revenue Code of 1954 or any successor provision thereto, and none of the said purposes shall at any time be deemed or construed to be purposes other than the public benefit purposes and objectives consistent with such educational and charitable status. *Bylaws, Article III*

PREFACE

NASPE's Secondary School Physical Education Council in September 1980 at its executive meetings identified this publication as one of many projects in the Council's five-year plan adopted in that year. The incentive and direction for this project stems from the success of the 1976 book, *Ideas for Secondary School Physical Education*, to which this publication is a sequel.

While the 1976 book focused on some of the revised and innovative teaching strategies and curricular programs of the 1970s in physical education, the present publication's major purpose is to help the practicing teacher through sharing and adapting teaching practices of other colleagues who are in the field today. By definition, an idea is nothing more than a presentation of sense or concept—a visible representation of a product. Thus, the ideas presented in this publication may not necessarily be original or innovative but are the result of teaching practices that may stimulate other ideas or "new wrinkles" for teachers of physical education to adopt and use within their own school setting. Possibly, more important to the reader of this publication is the notion that ideas evolve out of the teacher's personal perceptions and experiences. Thus, to this end, the teaching and curriculum practices disseminated throughout this book may or may not have relevance for some readers but certainly these ideas have the potential for relevance.

And, finally, it is entirely possible that some readers will evaluate their own teaching practices against the content of this book and will find that they are especially creative and innovative in certain areas. This is good! Such readers will then have the opportunity to become future contributing authors, sharing ideas with others. Ideas and Ideas II should lead to Ideas III. All physical educators should share with a purpose for the future.

Acknowledgments: The editor of this publication extends special appreciation to the 1980–83 members of the Secondary School Physical Education Council, whose assistance and identification of both ideas and authors facilitated the preparation of this book. Gratitude is especially due to Dianne O'Brien, Suzi D'Annolfo, Charlene Thomas, Don Hellison, Chick Hungerford, Tom Templin, and Diana Wells.

Furthermore, gratitude is extended to all of the contributing authors and to those who submitted programs. The editor wishes to thank all who shared ideas to use in teaching physical education and sports.

Ronald P. Carlson
Editor

CONTENTS

IDEAS II

PART I
CURRICULUM
IDEAS
Concepts
and
Designs

A Model Adaptive Physical Education Program

Submitted by: Dr. Dean Austin

School: Lincoln Public Schools
P.O. Box 82889
Lincoln, NE 68501

Summary

Remedial physical education can sometimes promote functional rehabilitation. This is, however, only a small part of a student's comprehensive educational program and should not be regarded as a total solution for abnormal functioning. Weak upper body muscles, for example, will not be strengthened solely by the establishment of strength-building exercises to be taught to all junior high school students. Physical educators must develop the whole person—interests, attitudes, motor skills, and physical prowess. To express physical education only in terms of remediation and rehabilitation is a mistake.

Physical educators must identify the needs of children and youth and clarify the needs of healthy, well-adjusted adults. Recent increases in nervous and mental diseases should encourage physical educators to design programs that strengthen the basal centers of the nervous system. The developmental physical education program at Irving Junior High School is designed to reintroduce enjoyable physical activities to somewhat sedentary youth. Its major goal is the motivation of sedentary students to greater participation. They must be made to feel that no day is complete without physical education activities.

Outline

I. Student selection
II. Identification of motor discrepancy
III. Remediation prescription
IV. Evaluation

Description

Three separate classifications for students who are scheduled in special classes are: (1) students with permanent disabilities that do not allow them to participate successfully in regular physical education classes; (2) students with temporary disabilities that do not allow them to participate successfuly in regular physical education classes; (3) students with severe motor discrepancies that make successful participation in a particular unit in regularly scheduled physical education classes impossible.

Students were initially identified for the developmental physical education class at Irving Junior High School after an extensive subjective evaluation by the four physical educators and one nurse involved in the program. Those identified were primarily students who performed poorly in the usual physical education classes. As a result, students with severe cardiac and respiratory problems, complicated orthopedic conditions, extreme obesity, and clumsiness comprised the first group. After consultation with parents and physicians, many of these students were assigned to the adapted class on a semester-to-semester basis and remained in the unit throughout the semester. Classes are currently limited to 12 students. Class size in the future will depend on the productivity of these classes.

Students temporarily assigned were also subjectively identified by the school physical educators because they were unable to perform specific sports skills. They were expected to be in the special class for between one week and one month. A temporary student may have a specific skills problem—such as poor eye-hand coordination—that prevents him or her from catching or dribbling a basketball; such a student may be assigned to the developmental class for an extensive program of sequential progressive activities designed to improve eye-hand coordination. Other students temporarily assigned to the adaptive class were those with handicaps of a temporary nature, such as those recovering from operations, long illnesses, or injuries.

After the physical educators identified program participants, parents and physicians of those students were sent letters developed by the Lincoln-Lancaster County Medical Society Educational Advisory Committee and the Physical Education Consultant of the Lincoln Public Schools. Physicians played leading roles in the actual assignment of students to the devel-

opmental physical education class. They also provided the prescriptive information used by the physical educator to design an individual activity program for each student.

The actual assignment of the students to the adaptive physical education class was then based on the cooperative judgment of the physician and the physical educator. The physician determined student limitations and capacities from a medical perspective. The physical educator and the physician interpreted these factors in terms of the appropriate student activity level, which in turn provided a general operational framework for prescribed exercises and activities. Whenever possible, it is best to have physician approval of general activity levels. For this reason, the letter to the physician listed mild, moderate, and unlimited physical education activities. Time was included for remedial exercises and sports and recreational skills.

Students with temporary disabilities (broken limbs, post-operative recovery) were scheduled in the class until released by the physician for participation in a regular program.

Conditions Specific to Program

The lesson for each particular class period evolves out of a teaching unit (i.e., ball skills) and is then based on activity progressions in an increasing order of difficulty. Class periods are arbitrarily divided into four activity parts, and lesson plans are developed correspondingly.

1. *Warm-ups (5 minutes)*

Warm-ups are conducted as a group activity and are designed to satisfy the student's initial need for activity at the start of the physical education class. The warm-ups also prepare the body for the movements that come later in the class period. Two-person exercises and stretching constitute a large part of the warm-ups.

2. *Individual Prescriptive Exercises (10–15 minutes)*

Each student receives an exercise program specifically designed for remediation of a physical disorder. This phase of the program is carefully planned to change each routine every two weeks, resulting in the equivalent of designing 12 different exercise programs every other weekend. Although earlier routines are reused as the year progresses, the program has sufficient variety to motivate the student and maintain interest in physical education classes.

3. *Instructional Phase (15–20 minutes)*

A brief review of the past lesson begins this phase of the day's instruction. Skill instruction is presented in a sequential progression within a teaching unit. Progressions are based on the abilities and progress of the majority of the group.

4. *Games or Relays (5–10 minutes)*

During this time a low-organized game, relay, or lead-up game is conducted that emphasizes the skills learned during the day's instructional phase. Sometimes this activity may be unrelated to the day's lesson and designed for a maximum amount of movement or just conducted to enjoy it. On certain days, this part of the day's activities is deleted and the time is given to further class instruction.

Evaluation

All children and youth have basic needs and benefit from normal developmental experiences. Their physical limitations sometimes make it necessary to provide certain protective measures while these needs are being met. Although this has been true in all levels of education, elementary grades and senior high schools have done much better than others in meeting such needs. It does not matter whether or not a program in physical education for exceptional populations is integrated, segregated, or a combination of the two. What matters is that (1) the students' needs and interests remain paramount, and (2) the physical educator remembers that safe and successful participation in physical education activities can have a greater impact on the total development of the adaptive student than that of any other school activity.

"Early Bird" Physical Education

Submitted by: Dr. Kenneth McGonagle
Ann Stevens

School: Evanston Township High School
1600 Dodge Ave.
Evanston, IL 60204

Summary

Three of the problems that continually arise at Evanston Township High School in planning and organizing the physical education curriculum for juniors and seniors are:
1. To be able to offer activities for which there is an interest but for which the demand is not sufficient to offer classes throughout the day.
2. To provide a schedule that will enable students:
   a. to leave school early for work experience;
   b. to arrange their schedule so that they may take an additional elective; or
   c. to take an extra gym class to make up a previous failure.
3. To offer lifetime sports that are of current interest to students but for which the school does not have facilities.

To solve these problems, an "early bird" physical education class is offered to juniors and seniors. As a general rule, this class meets before the normal school day begins (before 8:15 a.m.).

Outline

    I. Curriculum
   II. Fees
  III. Organization
  IV. Procedure
   V. Staffing

Description

The department chairmen, along with the staff, decide on the "early bird" curriculum on the basis of interest and available facilities. Two activities are offered in each unit, of which one may be off-campus. A student may elect to take an "early bird" class for one unit or up to the entire semester in place of the normally scheduled physical education class. Off-campus classes meet three days a week from 7:00 a.m. to 8:00 a.m. Classes on-campus meet from 7:15 a.m. to 8:00 a.m. daily, including dressing time.

Four units are offered each semester, each 4½ weeks in length.

First semester units

    I. Tennis or water games
    II. Folk dance or racquetball
    III. Ice skating or gymnastics
    IV. Roller skating or racquetball

Second semester units

    V. Conditioning (weight training and jogging) or ice skating
    VI. Fencing or Nautilus
    VII. Archery or racquetball
    VIII. Tennis or sailing

In arranging activities for which the school does not have facilities, the department chairmen contact managers of community facilities to arrange for classes and to set fees (if required). The fees usually include equipment and tend to average about $2.00 per session. Off-campus sessions normally meet 13 times for one hour each time. The department chairmen arrange for the school van or recreational department bus to return students to school at the completion of class.

A form describing the courses, listing any fees required, and other information is distributed to junior and senior students at the beginning of the first semester and again at the end of the first semester. Students register in the physical education office with the secretary. Classes are filled on a first-come basis. Any fee is paid at the time of registration. The parent's signature is required, alerting the parent that the student will be taking "early bird" physical education.

Classes such as racquetball and exercise on Nautilus equipment have a maximum number of 24 students, and other classes may have a maximum of 40. Classes of less than 15 are canceled, and students remain in their regularly scheduled physical education class.

Lists of students in the "early bird" classes are distributed to the physical education teachers so that those students are not marked absent from their normally sched-uled physical education classes. Grades and attendance are given to the regular teacher by the "early bird" teacher at the end of each unit. Grading is done on the same criteria as those used in the regular classes.

The department chairmen are assigned to the "early bird" physical education period. They teach the class or exchange classes with another teacher; for example, as racquetball is a very popular activity among the teachers, there is great demand from the staff to teach this class.

Conditions Specific to Program

All students are required to take daily physical education for four years. There are eight 45-minute periods in the day. Freshmen and sophomores have a core curriculum, while juniors and seniors have their choice of activities. Student enrollment is 3,500.

Evaluation

"Early bird" classes on campus have few space limitations, enabling students to participate under ideal conditions.

Some off-campus courses (for example, racquetball) have limited enrollment because of lack of available facilities.

The "early bird" curriculum is flexible and easily adaptable to meet the needs of the students. Staff members enjoy it because it offers them a chance to expand their interests and skills. The popularity of the program has encouraged other departments in the school to consider offering courses at this time of day.

Use of community facilities has enabled the department to expand the curriculum and offer activities that the students would not otherwise have an opportunity to experience. It has promoted goodwill in the community, and in many cases the students have continued to participate on their own.

Elective Physical Education

Submitted by: Rod Phillips

School: East High School
2800 E. Pershing Blvd.
Cheyenne, WY 82001

Summary

Primarily, physical education should be and can be fun. With this objective in mind, the needs and wants of the students can be met—providing exercise for all, as well as fun—through the institution of an elective physical education program. As students become older, they desire and choose to participate in activities in which they are interested and for which they have some talent. When they are interested, juniors and seniors participate vigorously and enthusiastically on their own, with self-direction and discipline—important factors in maturing and sportmanship.

Two other factors that are helpful in an elective program are a good required program for sophomores and a student leader program. In the required sophomore physical education program, East High School offers 25–30 activities. A student is exposed to these activities for one or two weeks, so that he can choose for the elective program those activities that are enjoyable and that can be performed with some proficiency.

The student leader program is open only to seniors who have completed two full years of physical education. They are selected by the department and give invaluable help.

Outline

I. Staffing
II. Support
III. Teacher-student interaction and co-operation

Description

The staff members should be of a congenial nature as well as being hard-working. At or near the end of each school year, the members of the department should meet to discuss and schedule areas of student interest and activity for the following year. Advance preparation enables the staff to overcome difficulties in scheduling, meeting needs, providing equipment, etc.

At first, all students are grouped together throughout the day's schedule. Each time a new activity is introduced, the up-perclass students are re-subjected to the presentation so that the new students may benefit. Through full administrative backing, a flexible and fair daily schedule has been established. There are now both an elective and a required program. Students have the option of enrolling for one or two semesters of the elective program.

Both instructors and students are involved, because the elective program relies on a give-and-take basis. The elective program is run mostly on a competitive basis, utilizing round-robin and double-elimination tournaments. Each student is responsible for picking up his own accountability card (see below) from the physical education office on the day of activity change. This accountability card is then taken to the instructor in charge of the activity and is kept on file until the final grade is given. Thus, each time a student picks up the card, he will be able to check on the grades received for previous activities.

Conditions Specific to Program

Sophomore Required Class
(First Semester)
1. Swimming
2. Softball
3. STX game
4. Team handball (boys only)
5. Field hockey (girls only)
6. Speedball and soccer (boys only)
7. Badminton (girls only)
8. Basketball
9. New games
10. Tumbling
11. Weights and conditioning
12. Jump rope and agility
13. Water polo and water polo in tubes
14. Dance
15. Rhythms and aerobics

Elective Physical Education
(First semester example)
Three weeks:
Outdoor education and survival
Team handball
Free swim
Softball
Golf
Bicycling
Project Adventure

Three weeks:
Badminton
Flag football (boys only)
Field hockey (girls only)
Archery
Weights and conditioning
Outdoor education and survival
Project Adventure

Evaluation

Strengths
1. Students choose an activity because of interest or ability.
2. Three weeks in each activity gives student time to develop skill.
3. Accountability card shows student the grades.

Name: John, Randy					Class: 12th	
Unit	Activity	Instructor		E	S	P
1	Team handball	Unger		A	B	C
2	Free swim	Phillips		A		A
3	Water polo	Phillips		A	A	A
4						

Grading: E—Effort   S—Team or individual standing (tournament play)
P—Participation (Every student starts with A and goes down for each day absent.)

Accountability Card

4. A program of three or four activities for the year is a thing of the past.

Weaknesses
1. The instructor must spend a great deal of time in preparation, pairing, scheduling, timing, and officiating, along with the construction and repair of equipment necessary for all the activities.
2. The elective program requires 4–6 staff members.

Physical Education for the Small School System

Submitted by: Gary M. Olson

School: Panama Central School
Panama, NY 14767

Summary

The physical education program at Panama Central School has undergone dramatic changes over the last few years as the result of many factors, including new state guidelines for physical education, Title IX, and staff initiative. Through imaginative utilization of resources and manipulation of student scheduling, the number and quality of physical education experiences possible for each student have been significantly increased.

The curriculum at the senior high school level places primary emphasis on dual and single lifetime sports and activities. However, time is also spent in such areas as team sports, self-testing activities, and aquatics.

Description

Grades 9–12 are taught on a three-two swing schedule, i.e., they meet three days a week one semester and two days a week the second semester. The 40-week year is further divided into four ten-week sessions for which different class offerings are available. Each ten-week class session is considered a separate course in physical education and, therefore, at the end of each school year every student has four separate grades. At the end of a typical high school career, a student could conceivably have taken 16 different courses from the department. Where possible, three different classes are offered during each period and students may elect the class they wish to take, subject to the following order of election: seniors and juniors; sophomores; and, finally, freshmen. This election, in effect, gives the student more instructional latitude.

An example of this system is a ten-week session in which tennis, golf, and archery might be offered. Students formally request these classes in the order of their preference, and then the staff tries to put them into the class they desire. The additional possibility of electing to take optional classes during the school day is available to the student when individual schedules permit. There are always several students taking more than one class during any ten-week session. Students in grades 10–12 are also given the option of taking classes in instructional physical education activities outside the school in lieu of regularly scheduled classes. For example, a student might be enrolled in a modern dance class at the YWCA or be taking skiing lessons at one of the local ski resorts. These requests must have the approval of the physical education staff and the Board of Education.

Students are also given the opportunity to apply for formal exclusion from regularly scheduled physical education classes while they are participating in interscholastic athletics, provided that they have demonstrated adequate proficiency in the activity from which they are being excused and that they scored a minimum 70th percentile level on all items of the most recent President's Council's Physical Fitness Test. Eligibility lists, posted at the start of each new school year, are based on the scores of the last fitness test given. Exclusions are not automatic but are subject to approval by physical education, guidance, and administrative staff.

Basic swimming is required of all students as a prerequisite for graduation. Instruction and testing are largely completed by the end of the eighth-grade year, but any student failing to meet minimum requirements by that time is automatically scheduled into all subsequent basic swimming courses until the deficiency is corrected.

This past year, the staff devised a cumulative record card for senior high school students. This card is part of the student's permanent records on file in the guidance office and is regularly forwarded along with other credentials for student profiles to various institutions and the military services. The card contains a complete listing of all courses (10-week classes) taken during high school, along with the name of the instructor and the subsequent grade. In addition to this information, a four-year profile of the student's performances on the President's Council's Youth Fitness Test is included, as well as a section for general comments. The addition of this system of accounting has added a long-needed dimension of credibility to the program.

Conditions Specific to Program

Traditional scheduling and facilities are sufficient to implement this program.

Sample Schedule

YEAR 1	2	3	4
First Ten Weeks			
A. Speedball	A. Golf	A. Speedball	A. Field hockey
B. Field hockey	B. Boating and hunter's safety	B. Archery	B. Running for fitness and aerobics
C. Archery	C. Soccer	C. Floor hockey	C. Soccer
Second Ten Weeks			
A. Basic swimming	A. Recreational swimming	A. Basic swimming	A. Recreational swimming
B. Volleyball	B. Recreational games	B. Basketball	B. Bowling
C. Weights and fitness	C. Weights and fitness	C. Cross-country skiing	C. Weights and fitness
Third Ten Weeks			
A. Lifesaving	A. Competitive swimming	A. Lifesaving	A. Synchronized swimming
B. Gymnastics	B. Power volleyball	B. Handball	B. Recreational games
C. Weights and fitness	C. Weights and fitness	C. Weights and fitness	C. Gymnastics
Fourth Ten Weeks			
A. Bowling	A. Tennis	A. Golf	A. Tennis
B. Softball	B. Softball	B. Softball	B. Softball
C. Handball and ping pong	C. Basic fishing	C. Squash	C. Camping

Evaluation

The program is a dynamic one and is constantly subjected to process or formative evaluation. It will periodically be subjected to summative evaluation. It is hoped that it will expand as better ways are found to meet the needs of both students and community.

Strengths
1. Wide range of instructional possibilities

2. Student election of classes, thus improving class morale
3. Teaching by instructors in their areas of greatest strength
4. Greater accountability and credibility

Weakness
Greatly increased record-keeping and administrative responsibilities.

Required High School Physical Education

Submitted by: Scott K. Evans

School: Eldorado High School
11,300 Montgomery N.E.
Albuquerque, NM 87111

Summary

Eldorado High School's approach to required physical education solves a number of universal problems, including:

1. Lack of program direction (philosophy, goals, objectives)
2. Low accountability (poor evaluation techniques, lack of course content, inflated grades)
3. Poor staff relationships (male-female, sharing of facilities and equipment, grading consistency)
4. Poor teacher and student morale and motivation
5. Same old traditional activities
6. Student experience dependent upon the individual section teacher

The program described here is called Physical Education Concepts and Activities. It has a positive impact on the above problem areas, as well as a number of coincidental positive outcomes.

Outline

I. Direction—philosophy
II. Base groups
III. Concepts unit
IV. Activity groups
V. Grading

Description

Direction and Philosophy

The program has a philosophy and related objectives that provide direction for the entire program (both the required course and electives):

Dimension 1—Physical Education Concepts
The students will learn a number of concepts dealing with physical activity and its effects on the body and total fitness.

Dimension 2—Physical Education Activities
The students will learn the skills and knowledges associated with a number of physical education activities. The student will attain a higher degree of total fitness.

Dimension 3—Physical Education Attitudes
The students will develop a positive attitude toward total fitness and activities that will help them attain it.

The required physical education course is important because it provides the bulk of the staffing, and it is the last required physical education experience. The description for this basic required course states that all students will complete Physical Education Concepts and Activities. This course includes: (1) successful completion of a written concepts test, (2) an increase in physical fitness, and (3) the attainment of an intermediate (traditional activities) or beginning (new activities) level of skill and knowledge in seven physical education activities.

The elective program description states that also students may elect other course offerings on completion of the basic course. The purpose of these offerings will be: (1) to further develop total fitness, or (2) to attain an advanced level of skill and knowledge in one or more physical education activities.

The required program should be the most important phase of the total high school program. Many, if not most, programs work backward from the elective program. Each teacher's favorite course is scheduled and then the required program consists of the remaining activities, facilities, and equipment. The required course should be planned first, and the elective program should then be developed.

Base Groups

Students are assigned by computer to co-educational base groups or sections of the required course in Physical Education Concepts and Activities. The base teacher, in cooperation with a counterpart male or female staff member, is responsible for locker assignments, as well as for the concepts unit, fitness testing, and grade averaging and reporting.

Concepts Unit

Following orientation and locker assignments, the base groups move into the fitness concepts unit, which lasts approximately 20 school days. At the beginning of the unit, the AAHPERD Health-Related Fitness Test is administered, with follow-up tests at the end of each semester.

The fitness concepts material is broken down into approximately 18 general concepts, including flexibility, health-related aspects, skill-related aspects, exercise and weight control, nutrition, sports injuries, cardiovascular fitness, etc.

The concepts unit and materials are teacher-developed from resource materials and are standardized for all teachers and sections of Physical Education Concepts and Activities. The materials include handouts for each student giving terms and facts relating to each concept plus ideas and materials for the teacher. Teaching stations are rotated during the unit, and the base teacher has the responsibility of planning activities that relate to that day's concept (e.g., 12-minute run for the cardiovascular fitness concept). At the end of the unit, a standardized test is given to all sections.

With effective instruction, the objectives of Dimension 1—Physical Education Concepts should be accomplished on completion of the year's first unit, which is fitness concepts.

Activity Groups

The rest of the year is divided into seven units of approximately 20–22 school days (two units each 45-day grading period). The activities offered are selected on the basis of their contribution to total fitness. They may be developmental activities that will give the student the experience of working to attain fitness (e.g., weight training, wrestling, gymnastics). They may be activities that contribute to social-emotional fitness (e.g., golf and archery). They may also be lifetime activities that contribute to fitness now and may be continued later in life (e.g., tennis, aerobic dance, volleyball). These seven units are designed to meet the objectives of Dimension 2—Physical Education Activities.

Choice Day. The first day of each activity unit is called choice day. This is a mini-registration for each class period. If there are five base groups or sections, then five different activities may be offered, such as wrestling, flag football, basketball, soccer, and volleyball.

Teacher Assignment. Teachers are assigned to activities according to their expertise and interest. Each activity has a coordinator who is responsible for skills progressions, handouts, tests, etc. This provides some standardization across the program (different teachers, same activity) and minimizes planning time by avoiding duplication of effort. There is enough flexibility in the assignment of teachers to provide expert instruction and, at the same time, to avoid teacher boredom from teaching the same activity all day.

Student Assignment. The base teacher keeps a choice card for each base student. These cards are passed out at the beginning of the period on choice day. The card has the student's name, grade, student number, base teacher, and section number listed at the top. The body of the card has space to write in each activity and activity teacher for the seven units. Tables are set up, with each teacher seated behind a sign indicating the activity he or she is teaching for the upcoming unit. Students are called up by base groups to select the activity they desire. To enroll, they merely turn in their choice card to the activity teacher. The activity teacher then makes out an activity roll sheet from the cards received, noting the teacher's name and the activity on the choice cards and returning them to the base teacher. In this way students are prevented from signing up for the same activity twice. The card also provides a ready reference for the base teacher to locate students when necessary. The order of choice is rotated by base groups. The more popular activities (e.g., racquetball, weight lifting, etc.) are offered more than once during the year. Small group activities such as tennis are balanced with large group activities such as track. This allows for effective instruction in activities where facilities, equipment, and skills necessitate a smaller number of students.

The delivery of these units in a positive way (i.e., teacher expertise and enthusiasm, choices in selection of activities, variation of classmates and teachers, and generally improved student and teacher morale) fulfills the objectives of Dimension 3—Physical Education Attitudes.

Grading

The base teacher is responsible for the averaging and reporting of 9-week and semester grades. The activity teacher is responsible for the reporting of an activity unit grade and attendance information. Each unit grade *must* include at least one skill grade and one written grade. All grades are recorded as percentage scores. All teachers use the same key for recording days absent, days tardy, etc. The activity teacher makes copies of his or her activity roll and grade sheet and passes them on to the base teachers at the end of each activity unit. The base teachers note the unit grades from the activity sheets and average the two unit grades for a 9-week grade and average the two 9-week grades for a semester grade.

Conditions Specific to Program

This program requires a commitment on the part of every staff member. Each person is dependent upon the other for deadlines and grading procedures. There is also a great deal of clerical work involved in recording choices and recording and reporting grades.

This program also requires a great deal of advance planning on the part of the department chairperson, who must develop the concepts unit, plan a rotation of facilities for the fitness testing and concepts unit, and develop the activity schedule for the entire year. Individual staff members may volunteer or be assigned to help with these tasks.

Evaluation

Strengths
1. Objective evaluation
2. Staff cooperation
3. Effort required by all staff members
4. Consistent direction for students
5. Improved student morale and motivation

6. Improved teacher morale and motivation
7. Accountability
8. Fitness concepts component included
9. Opportunity for small group instruction
10. Standardization among teachers

Weaknesses
1. Need for a great deal of advance planning
2. Commitment from every staff member

3. Need for a great deal of clerical work

General Comments

This program has a tremendous impact on staff cooperation and effort. The system has its own set of checks and balances to insure that every staff member pulls his or her own weight. Both the consistency of effort and the required cooperation result in better instruction for each student in each class in each activity.

Advanced Physical Education Without Increasing Staff

Submitted by: Marlowe Mullen

School: Greenwood Community High
School
615 Smith Valley Road
Greenwood, IN 46142

Summary

Many schools do not offer their students a major or a minor in physical education. This is unfortunate for students who may wish to continue their education beyond high school in this field of study. As in all educational disciplines, there is always a need for good teachers.

A variety of reasons are given by administrators for not offering a major or minor in the field of physical education. Among those reasons are:

1. Only two (or four) semesters of physical education are required, and each semester is worth only a half credit.
2. In order to offer enough classes in physical education to earn a major or minor, there would have to be a "phase elective" program available all four years, requiring an increase in staff at a time when most schools are experiencing a reduction in force.
3. The school does not have the facilities to increase physical education offerings.

This article presents basic information about the method used at Greenwood High School to eliminate these problems and at the same time make a physical education major available to all students. Specific details for each phase of the elective program are included in the two articles following this one.

Outline

I. Staffing an advanced program
II. Scheduling an advanced program
III. Coordination of facilities
IV. Full-credit proposal to administration
V. Scope of program in relation to available facilities off school grounds

Description

Setting up a meaningful advanced physical education program which can offer students as many additional semesters or years of physical education as they wish to take requires only one person in the department who has at least one free period available.

To make this an advanced class, it is best to reserve it for upperclassmen who have successfully completed the required physical education classes. For some schools, this would mean a change in scheduling so that all students finish the required classes during their freshman and sophomore years, thus leaving their junior and senior years for the elective programs.

One other scheduling consideration for this program is the time of day that it is offered. Because of the nature of some of the activities and because most upperclassmen have more free time in the afternoon, it is advantageous to offer this class as late in the day as possible.

It is not an easy task for the instructor, but one person can develop two separate courses of study that do not repeat what has been offered in the required classes and that do not repeat themselves. These courses are taught by the same instructor in alternate years. Once this schedule is set up, a student may take the advanced class in the junior and senior years and may earn credit for both years without repeating the same course. Under this plan, no additional staff is required and no additional facilities are used. The instructor must coordinate the advanced class curriculum with the required class curriculum, in order to utilize the same facility all day even though the activities may not be the same.

One other factor stands in the way of students who wish to earn a major in physical education. Each state requires a certain number of credits to qualify for a major in any subject. Since many states (or schools) give only half a credit for physical education, it becomes burdensome for students to try and earn a major. The final, and perhaps the most difficult, task for the instructor is to develop a curriculum that, in the eyes of administration, is worthy of a full credit. In Greenwood Community High School this phase was not attempted until the courses had been taught for two years, so that the proposal could include examples of a student major's work as well as staff rationale for the change.

Conditions Specific to Program

In the four required semesters of physical education, Greenwood Community High School offers most of the activities that the facilities will permit. In setting up the advanced class curriculum, an endeavor was made to broaden the scope of physical education and explore many of the opportunities available outside of the gymnasium. Some of these activities require the use of a classroom, and others require the use of community facilities.

If the school is within three miles of any public facilities, the instructor should explore the possibility of utilizing them for advanced classes. If there are several available, it will be advantageous to become licensed to drive a school bus.

This type of program lends itself well to a coeducational setting. There are no competitive sports played in this program, and the classes do not have skill tests over the units that are taught. The specifics of grading are explained in more detail in the two articles following this one.

Evaluation

Maintaining the academic integrity of this course can cost it much of its growth potential. The amount of paperwork required of the students must be carefully weighed to make certain that it is significant and not just busy work. This class can be the highlight of the instructor's day and of the student's high school experience if handled properly.

Advanced Physical Education, An Alternative: Year One

Submitted by: Marlowe Mullen

School: Greenwood Community High
School
615 Smith Valley Road
Greenwood, IN 46142

Summary

This is the second of three articles dealing with the expanding of a physical education program, without necessitating additional staff or facilities. As a result, students have the opportunity to earn a major or minor and gain a greater understanding of what physical education encompasses.

This article summarizes the first year of the advanced physical education class at Greenwood Community High School. It was developed eight years ago, after recognizing that students perceived their advanced class activities as "the same old thing" even though advanced skills were being taught.

The program is based on the following five objectives:
1. To broaden the scope of physical education activities
2. To do away with traditional competitive methods of evaluating students according to performance
3. To give students an opportunity to explore some activities from a different perspective (e.g., teaching, officiating, etc.)
4. To allow students an opportunity to research any physical education or sports-related activity they wish to explore (in written form)
5. To regenerate an interest in physical education and lifetime activities.

Outline

I. Coordination of facilities
II. Activities
III. Grading

Description

As mentioned in the preceding article, it is important for the person teaching the advanced class to coordinate the activities of all his classes so that the same facility can be used all day, even though the activities are different. This takes time and thought before the school year begins. Proposals should be given to the department head as soon as possible to help avoid conflicts with other staff members.

To determine which activities or units will be included, an inventory of all area facilities should be taken—i.e., facilities in about a three-mile or four-mile radius. The yellow pages may help or, better yet, students can be asked what is available. There is always the possibility of teaching an activity in the classroom and then taking a long field trip to try out the activity.

The following are some activities that have been taught or are still being taught in this program:

1. *Aerobics:* Students jog in the neighborhood, not around a track (a bus can be waiting to take them back). They do speed skating at the local roller skating facility for 15 minutes. They can do something other than running five days a week, such as racquetball, lap swimming, rope jumping, or even a day of fast walking in the neighborhood. Conditioning can be interesting.

2. *Athletic training:* After emphasizing the modalities, injury evaluation, and rehabilitation, a field trip is taken to the nearest and best training room in the area, such as a local college, a private sports medicine clinic, or the facility used by the nearest professional sports team.

3. *Attack prevention:* This is an awareness program of problems and solutions. Films, local police agency speakers, county prosecutors, etc., are resources.

4. *Bicycling:* In the classroom, students learn bicycle safety, cycling technique, and bicycle maintenance. This should take as much time as necessary for the students to repair their bicycles and make them ready for a safety inspection. As soon as all bicycles have passed the inspection, the remaining time is spent in riding in the community. Students map the course that the class will take. Their routes usually go past some refreshment option, but in promoting lifetime activities it is important to give the students a positive feeling so that they will be more inclined to participate on their own.

5. *Bowling:* Students bowl as much as possible, but each student must learn how to keep score by the end of the unit. Most bowling establishments provide some free

instruction, which should be used to advantage.

6. *First aid:* The most common first aid procedures, such as stopping bleeding, cardiopulmonary resuscitation (CPR), and the Heimlich Maneuver, are reviewed. In addition to these and others, the procedures to be taken at the scene of an accident are explained. As many of these students will be parents in the next several years and one of the most common causes of death in children is poisoning, procedures for such emergencies are also reviewed.

7. *Gymnastics:* This is an opportunity to explore one of the many avenues of physical education, as well as to help prepare students for parenthood. In this unit one week is spent in the classroom talking about preschool-age children: physical, emotional, and social development, need for tactile security, etc. During the second week the students teach gymnastics (basic body awareness stunts) to preschool-age children.

8. *Leadership training:* During this program each student teaches the class two games. Games are chosen by the students from a list provided by the instructor. At the end of this unit, each student must compile a card catalog of all of the games presented. Each card must have the rules of the game on one side and a diagram on the other side. After grading, these cards are kept by the students for future use.

9. *Markmanship:* Gun safety is taught first, using local National Rifle Association personnel or law enforcement resources to explain procedures, safety, and the laws pertaining to firearms. Air guns (rifles and/or pistols) are used to teach markmanship.

10. *Motorcycle safety:* The local motorcycle retailer sends people out to teach this. They cover equipment, riding procedures, maintenance, local laws, and the procedures for deciding what type of motorcycle best fits a person's needs. At the end of this course, two or three days are spent riding small motorcycles (provided by the retailer), so that students who have never ridden can master the braking and shifting methods.

11. *Officiating:* Some of the fundamentals of officiating that are common to most sports are taught. It is best to make up a new game so that no student will have an advantage over others. Students study the rules of the game and the techniques of officiating in the classroom and then take turns refereeing the game. At the end of each game segment, the instructor reviews what has been done, pointing out strengths and weaknesses.

12. *Physiology of exercise:* The focus is on items which the students can relate to their own situations, such as the overload principles, how the body uses sugar, atrophy vs. hypertrophy, fatigue theories, psychological vs. physiological limits, and response of the muscles to isotonic vs. isometric exercises.

13. *Speleology:* Caving safety is taught, as well as proper equipment used for caving, speleogenesis, and cave conservation. A member of the National Speleological Society in the area could help to teach the class. The unit ends with a field trip (all day) to a local cave (about 80 miles from school).

14. *Training comparisons:* The instructor tries to prove or disprove the theory of specificity of training to the class in the weight room. Students work in pairs. Each pair selects an exercise or muscle group which they wish to improve. Each person in the pair has a different workout. The instructor points out which overload principle each student is using, referring to what they learned in physiology of exercise. Pretests and post-tests are conducted for each student for both strength and endurance. In a four-week unit, the results will be obvious.

Many of these subjects are at the perimeter of what most people consider as physical education. Many of these units are not within the expertise of the physical education instructor. This list was selected to demonstrate two things: (1) it is not necessary to limit physical education to the teaching and testing of sports skills (many of which will seldom, if ever, be used after graduation), and (2) it is not necessary to limit the students' scope of physical education to those topics which the instructors feel comfortable about teaching. Somewhere within the community there is a person with a thorough knowledge of any subject. It is essential to use those resources.

It is important to note that skills tests are not given on these activities. Each activity is presented in such a way that participation, along with minimum classroom work, will yield basic understanding and more interest.

The instructor in this program must be aware of students who show interest so that they can be given further instruction. A student turned off by too much "teaching" learns little, but the student who learns a little and asks to learn more because he sees fun or value in the subject often develops a contagious attitude.

During the first semester, each student is given a contract containing 13 individual assignments for written work pertaining to their chosen subject. Each assignment has a point value between 4 and 20 points. Students are to choose from the contract enough items to earn the grade they wish to receive. There are over 150 points available.

Papers are graded according to their individual worth (i.e., an item worth 15 points will receive 1–15 points, depending on content, form, grammar, spelling, etc.). The total of all the papers turned in by a student determines his grade according to the school's grading scale. If a student chooses to research a related subject which does not lend itself to the structured format of the contract, that student may fulfill the contract requirement by writing a traditional term paper.

For the first semester only, this written work is combined with a participation grade to determine the student's final grade. Students are given one week of class time in the library to help them find sources. This project encourages the use of library facilities, personal contact with professionals, and the use of sources of information which otherwise might never be sought.

Grading procedures for the second semester are altered slightly. Instead of a research project, students are given written tests over several of the units and a card file assignment, as explained above in the description of the leadership training unit. The student's semester grade is based on test scores, the card file, and participation in the various activities.

Conditions Specific to Program

It is useful to have a classroom available, since several units will involve some lecture situations. If off-campus facilities are available and the administration is in agreement, it is helpful to become licensed to drive the bus for class outings.

The most critical need in developing a new curriculum of this type is the ability to recognize new horizons for physical education. The instructor must also be willing to educate, as well as perform, and to approach everything in the class in as interesting a way as possible.

Evaluation

Strengths
1. Students are not penalized for lack of strength or skill.

2. The absence of competitive grading helps to develop an attitude of cooperation in the class.
3. Students do not constantly repeat activities which they have done in physical education before.
4. The requirements of the class are such that the administration should recognize the course as a full-credit offering.
5. Since the course is a full credit, students can earn a major or minor in physical education.
6. No new equipment or facilities are needed to develop an advanced program.

Weaknesses
1. Not all schools have public facilities available within a four-mile radius.
2. Not all corporations will allow off-campus activities on a daily basis, or have buses available for class use. (This had never been done until this course.)
3. Not all students care about earning a major or minor in physical education, and therefore the additional paperwork and classroom activities do not appeal to some.

Advanced Physical Education, An Alternative: Year Two

Submitted by: Marlowe Mullen

School: Greenwood Community
High School
615 Smith Valley Road
Greenwood, IN 46142

Summary

After changing our advanced skills class to the advanced physical education class described in the preceding article, it was offered to any upperclassman who had successfully completed four semesters of required physical education. Many of the students who took the class as a junior wanted to repeat the course as a senior. Unfortunately, they were told, "No, you have fulfilled the requirements for that class."

To solve this problem, without increasing staff or facilities, a new curriculum was developed. This new course was taught by the same instructor, alternating years with the existing course. Therefore, a student could take advanced physical education in both junior and senior years and not repeat the same course.

Outline

I. Establishing need
II. Course content
III. Grading

Description

A new curriculum was developed, based on the textbook *Fitness For Life* by Dr. Charles Corbin, Kansas State University, and Dr. Ruth Lindsey, California State University. The content of the book was tested and shown to offer information, presented in a concise and easy to understand manner, which students did not know after six semesters of physical education. Furthermore, it was found that a two-semester course could be developed, correlating various activities with the chapters of the text in such a way that students could study a type of fitness and develop that same type of fitness simultaneously.

The purpose of utilizing the book *Fitness For Life* is to give students the tools necessary for maintaining or regaining, at a later date, their youthful vitality. It is one thing to be healthy and strong in youth; it is entirely different to understand how to systematically and wisely develop that same condition once it is lost. *Fitness For Life* does this well. Students learn the vocabulary, the testing methods, and the activities that are necessary to develop the 11 parts of fitness presented in the book. The text is not geared to athletes but to the realization that each individual has individual fitness needs.

Simple testing methods are utilized that require no special equipment. Most items involve self-testing, which can be repeated on one's own time at a later date. Perhaps best of all, the student gains an understanding of himself and realizes that he can control how he looks, how he feels, and how he can change by using the simple principles learned in this book.

The goal of the text is to teach each student how to evaluate the various parts of fitness, to determine where weaknesses and strengths lie, and to set up a program of fitness which properly fits the needs of the individual.

The following list includes several of the subjects covered in *Fitness For Life*:

Threshold of training
   Principle of overload
   Principle of progression
   Principle of specificity
Cardiovascular fitness
Strength
Muscular endurance
Flexibility
Exercise and fat control
Exercise and good health
Balance
Agility
Coordination
Power
Speed
Reaction time
Correct way to exercise
Lifetime activities
Planning an exercise program
Attitudes about fitness

If the instructor wants to make the class goal-oriented, a fitness festival can be the culminating activity for the year. The following are some of the steps to consider in setting up such a festival:

1. Each student specializes in one area of fitness. That student should be able to answer questions about it, measure it, explain what the measurements indicate, and tell how to improve that part of fitness.
2. Students contact medical or research professionals who would be willing to give 30-minute to 40-minute lectures on various subjects dealing with fitness and health.
3. Students contact retailers who would be willing to set up displays to demonstrate fitness equipment and training methods.
4. Students contact local businesses to find a financial sponsor for the fitness festival. The sponsor's main concern should be to furnish publicity.
5. Students contact a local runner's club to organize a fun run on the day of the festival.
6. Students contact local health agencies (Heart Association, American Red Cross, Alcoholics Anonymous, etc.) to set up booths for the dispersment of free information, free blood pressure tests, etc.
7. Each student prepares an area to test people in a fitness specialty. The students will need national norms for a wide range of ages so that the information they give to the public is as accurate as possible.

It is sad to think that by the time young people are 17 and 18 years of age, very few have had an opportunity to decide what is best for themselves. In an effort to make this class more meaningful to the students, the instructor allows them to place values on their work according to their priorities.

There are four items of value in this class:

1. *The textbook:* Students are to keep their books up-to-date, filling in the self-testing sections and the testing sections at the appropriate times.

2. *Written quizzes:* Each week a quiz is given over the material covered for that week in the text.

3. *A notebook:* This is kept by each student for future reference and contains the following sections:
   a. Personal fitness profile

b. Vocabulary list (50 words per semester dealing with fitness)
c. Copies of articles that give information about an area of interest to the student
d. A description of each of the various fitness testing methods and the relative values of the test results (e.g., the step test and the values for Excellent, Good, etc.).
e. Evaluations of each of the activities and sports that the class participates in during the year (forms from the book)
f. All handouts

4. *Participation:* For each day a student does not participate in an activity, 2.45 percent of his grade is deducted. This means that for every three unexcused days, the student's grade for this section is lowered one letter.

At the beginning of the year, the students are allowed to give each of these four areas a value between 5 and 35 percent. The input for each category is averaged, and the percentages are rounded off to give a total value of 100 percent. Final grades are determined in accordance with these percentages.

Conditions Specific to Program

The facilities needed for this program are basic. The same areas used for other physical education classes during the day will be appropriate, but pre-planning is required to coordinate use of facilities. A classroom may be of use if some of the material is presented in lecture or film.

Evaluation

Care should be taken by the instructor not to load the students with too much paperwork in this course. The concepts can be learned quickly and demonstrated through various activities without necessitating an abundance of homework. The concepts of the various types of fitness should be integrated with the activities students choose to participate in. The instructor should point out to the students whenever possible how much a particular type of fitness is used in the activity they are trying. Learning through doing is much more interesting than learning by taking notes.

Quality Control of Secondary Physical Education Programs

Submitted by: Dr. John P. Bennett,
Supervisor*

School: Hanover County Public Schools
Ashland, VA 23005

Summary

In the fields of health, physical education and driver education at the Hanover County Public Schools, continuous efforts were always being made to upgrade the quality of the program. The checklist presented here was developed and used in all the secondary schools in the system. The form is slightly modified to reflect pursuits of lifetime activities and health-related fitness. The activities that appear on the checklist can be changed to meet local and future needs.

Outline

Presented below is a 36-week program checklist for secondary physical education

*Currently Assistant Professor, Health and Physical Education Department, George Mason University, Fairfax, Virginia 22030.

teachers. It is designed to assist them in providing the highest quality of instruction within their programs. The checklist can be used at any grade level, and it provides information to all those involved with the programs about the content of each program at any given time throughout the school year.

The chart is also designed to assist teachers in providing balanced programs in their schools. It provides each teacher with a visual record of the program on one sheet of paper. The teachers using this chart know exactly how many lessons were taught in each activity that they have presented during the course of the school year. This is a very helpful aid in determining possible weak and strong points of a curriculum and a teacher. It is also extremely helpful as input for any external or internal evaluation of a particular program.

At the bottom of the chart is a note reminding the teacher to send a copy to the principal and to the supervisor, so that a record is provided to everyone involved with the program. Information of this nature over the years is extremely helpful in program revision and growth.

Program Checklist for Secondary Physical Education

School Name _____

*Place a number in the appropriate weekly box for the number of lessons that week devoted to the activity.

GRADE _____

ACTIVITY	Week 1–36					
TEAM SPORTS	First	Second	Third	Fourth	Fifth	Sixth
Basketball						
Field hockey						
Flag football						
Floor hockey						
Lacrosse						
Soccer						
Softball						
Speedball/speedaway						
Team handball						
Volleyball						
Water Polo						
INDIVIDUAL/DUAL	First	Second	Third	Fourth	Fifth	Sixth
Archery						
Badminton						
Bicycling						
Bowling						
Camping						
Golf						
Gymnastics						
Handball						
Jogging						
Rhythmic gymnastics						
Personal fitness						
Racquetball						
Skating(roller/ice)						
Skiing(down/cross-country)						
Swimming						
Tennis						
Track and field						
Weight training						
Wrestling						
DANCE	First	Second	Third	Fourth	Fifth	Sixth
Aerobic dance						
Ballet						
Folk, round, and square dance						
Jazz						
Modern						
Social						

Week 1–36

Copy to: Principal
Supervisor
Teacher

Instructor's Signature _____

Conditions Specific to Program

By giving the local community an opportunity to see these charts, a good method of promoting positive school-community relations is developed. Since there is growing concern today about accounting for expenditures, this chart can be an excellent method for promoting quality use of community revenue in the physical education program.

One final value of this chart is its value to the physical education teacher personally. Each individual teacher can now see how to provide better and more balanced programs for students in the future.

Evaluation

Principals, supervisors, and teachers all agreed that this form has contributed greatly to a much higher quality in the program content of their physical education programs. Through the use of this form, a graphic picture of program content results. It should be noted that the activities listed on this chart need to be updated regularly in order to keep abreast of current trends. Outdoor pursuits or an outdoor education section, containing activities such as orienteering, adventure activities, and backpacking, would certainly be appropriate for inclusion.

The content of the chart is determined by the current curriculum. The use of such a chart may be the first step toward revitalizing, reshaping, and updating a program.

PART II
INSTRUCTIONAL IDEAS
Teaching Notions and Concepts

Using Organizational Development Techniques to Improve Teaching

Submitted by: Dr. Jack Hutslar
North American Youth
Sport Institute
4985 Oak Garden Drive
Kernersville, NC 27284

Summary

Much of the effort to improve teaching in workshops and at conferences is directed toward individual teachers. Seldom is the organization itself—the school system—viewed as the source of teacher ineffectiveness. Some organization-wide methods suggested to improve the quality of teaching in physical education include: (1) make physical education voluntary, (2) exclude coaches from teaching, and (3) make entrance standards for teachers more rigorous. These solutions overlook an important factor. Some teachers who are ineffective in the gymnasium are good teachers on the practice fields and courts. The problem with the quality of teaching in some systems is that teachers will not teach. The solution to this problem cannot be found in workshops and through inspirational talks.

In business and industry, just as in education, the performance of employees can become poor; workers are capable of doing well, but they do not do what is expected of them. This type of organization-wide problem can be addressed through organizational development techniques that stress process consultation. In process consultation, the teachers and administrators enter into joint meetings in broadly formed units for the purpose of (1) seeking changes, (2) making changes, (3) openly accepting the views of others without fear of reprisal, and (4) bargaining or compromising as needed to produce the most desirable changes that result in improved teaching.

Outline

I. Why poor teaching in physical education can exist
II. How organizational development techniques can improve the quality of teaching.

Description

Reasons for Poor Teaching

There are a number of recognized reasons why teachers of physical education may not do well in the instructional setting. The list below is not exhaustive, but it does explain in some part why physical education programs are often conducted by non-teachers.

1. *Teacher/coach role conflict.* Coaches neglect their teaching responsibilities in order to devote their time to those duties that provide them with job security and recognition.

2. *Teacher burnout.* The stress and anxiety of working in a physically demanding teaching situation has a negative influence on teaching performance.

3. *Bureaucratic organization.* Teachers and instructional objectives become secondary to the many other goals that must be met for the organization to continue functioning regularly.

4. *Organizational conflict.* When problems surface, they tend to be ignored and allowed to become worse. Interpersonal conflict can cause further unrest. When conflict is resolved through the use of dictatorial authority by the decision-makers (i.e., administrators), open conflict is only postponed.

5. *"Throw-out-the-ball" programs.* It is quite easy in physical education to give in to student requests or to present an endless series of pointless, noninstructional activities. In some cases, teachers who do teach feel pressure not to teach when they offer demanding, developmental courses of instruction.

6. *Expediency.* Teachers are given physical education teaching responsibilities when they are certified in other areas.

7. *Duties.* An endless series of demanding and tiring duties are required of physical education teachers. These custodial tasks (i.e., duty in the lunch room, locker room, study hall, and restrooms; bus duty; safety patrol; playground supervision; etc.) use time and energy that should be expended on serious teaching and on professional curiosity and growth.

8. *Absence of support.* The absence of school support from administrators and in-service programs (i.e., workshops, professional leave, aids, incentives for good

teaching) does not foster professional interest in good teaching.

9. *Income.* Teachers need second and third incomes to meet routine living expenses. The cost for professional development (i.e., books, conferences, and graduate courses) cannot be justified in lieu of a moderate quality of life enjoyed by most citizens.

10. *Admission to teaching.* A majority of teachers come from the bottom half of the college population. It may be that poor teaching is a result of the poor preparation of disinterested students.

Organizational Development

The purpose here is to give examples of how teachers, supervisors, and superintendents can use organizational development techniques to improve teaching. When changing physical education from noninstructional to instructional programs, massive changes may be required. In schools, as in industry, the intention is to eliminate something that is not supposed to occur (i.e., not teaching) and to replace it with what is supposed to occur (i.e., teaching). The problem has become the absence of teaching and the solution is a complete reorientation to the teaching process. It is one problem not to know how to teach; it is another problem to know how to teach and yet not teach.

In adopting an organizational development approach, particularly that referred to as process consultation, the system is examined by all of those involved with the program. This approach is recommended because it demands that all teachers and administrators work together to find or produce solutions to the problem of nonteaching. Those who meet must have the capacity and authority to make changes; otherwise, time and effort are wasted.

It is not the purpose of organizational development to get teachers to accept the wishes of administrators. All personnel meet in joint, cooperative sessions. Meetings can range from single interviews to broadly formed groups. They meet to seek change, make changes, openly accept the views of others without fear of reprisal, and bargain or compromise as needed to produce the most desirable changes that result in improved teaching. The following material is a brief sketch of how to bring about positive changes in the quality of teaching. Open communication and cooperation are key facets in the process.

Steps in Organizational Development

1. Evaluate the instructional program, formally or informally. Determine whether or where change is needed.

2. Convene a small committee of teachers and administrators who are willing to address problems in the quality of teaching. This may be a department, school, or system-wide project. It is essential for the long-term success of the process that teachers and administrators enter the meetings on equal footing. In some cases, one or more outside consultants or mediators may be employed to coordinate the process. This assures that all sides and points of view receive equal attention, consideration, and action.

3. Eventually form a variety of groups, both temporary and permanent, as needed. The participants discuss, review, examine, evaluate, and identify why nonteaching occurs. Specific groups or topics might include, but are not limited to, the following:
   a. The absence of, or the quality of, teaching in the system
   b. School climate
   c. Workloads
   d. Extra duties, both compensated and not compensated
   e. Equipment and facilities (including dungeon-like locker rooms and offices)
   f. Relationships among teachers, administrators, parents, students, and support people
   g. The curriculum, including course offerings and evaluation
   h. Being an up-to-date teacher and administrator
   i. A plan of action
   j. Implementing the plan
   k. Maintaining the quality of teaching over time

These meetings should be viewed not as opportunities to air grievances but as the means by which changes are made. They are conducted in open, intensive, fact-finding atmospheres with the administrative hierarchies of the school authority system cast aside. If one side is pitted against another, the process is almost certainly doomed to failure. Administrators, in particular, must be willing to shed their cloak of authority, accept criticism, and share in the blame. It is then that the staff can begin to identify what it is about the system that makes nonteaching possible, comfortable, more desirable than teaching, and the rule rather than the exception.

4. Form in-service, staff development, and training programs to reacquaint teachers and other staff members with the fundamentals of their respective professions. This may involve in-school and after-school workshops planned and conducted both by local teachers and outside authorities. Specific objectives of these workshops may be:
   a. To retrain teachers in their content or cognate areas as well as in new areas
   b. To learn new teaching methods and the latest research on teaching
   c. To assist in the planning of lessons and development of overall teaching strategies
   d. To monitor student and teacher achievement through standardized testing programs
   e. To adopt self-help plans where teachers can learn to monitor and improve their own performance
   f. To produce fully functioning teachers and administrators in three years
   g. To implement a preventive maintenance program or quality control system to assure that good teaching remains the rule and is the primary goal in the system.

5. In some cases, the motivation to improve teaching performance may come directly from the administrators. The business community has found that job enrichment, management by objectives (MBO), and

Theory Z management can stimulate performance. Job enrichment is a management strategy that provides employees with a variety of work experiences at high levels of personal responsibility. Management by objectives is adequately described as a motivational strategy; it is largely a variation of competency-based instruction. Objectives are developed through joint planning by teacher and supervisor. Theory Z management, so successful in Japanese business and industry, brings all employees together in quality control circles, where specific attention can be given to the products and the primary goals of the organization.

6. Most educators will recognize that teachers and teaching can receive additional support if certain structural changes are made in the system. Discussion and change will probably be suggested in these areas:

a. Schedules, class loads, duties, equipment, and facilities
b. Combatting one-sided use of power by administrators against staff members
c. Providing growth opportunities outside the school, so that teaching is not regarded as a "dead-end" job
d. Enriching the curriculum and resource materials for teachers
e. Giving teachers opportunities to participate in prestigious and status-raising activities, such as conducting responsible school tasks and delivering presentations that focus on teaching and learning
f. Establishing guest teacher, teacher exchange, master teacher, and clinical teacher programs
g. Ceasing to assign people to teach physical education when they have no desire or training to work in the area
h. Acknowledging good teaching, with teacher-of-the-week and teacher-of-the-month awards in each subject area—expanding this to area and regional recognition, featuring good programs of instruction in the local

media, and developing incentives or acknowledgments from a pool of corporate benefactors.

7. Once the organizational development process begins to influence the quality of teaching and school life in general, it would be prudent to establish one or more permanent structures or committees. They would be formed to monitor the system, as do quality control circles, and to maintain activities to assure that the quality of teaching remains uniformly high. Added groups or structures could include:

a. Resource centers
b. Audiovisual teaching studios
c. Teacher aides and assistants
d. Independent counselor-consultants for teacher assistance
e. Job opportunity, school governance, and teacher-administrator liaison groups
f. Committee on quality of teaching

8. Gymnasiums and accompanying facilities must become places where a positive atmosphere about working, teaching, and learning can exist. Physical education teachers require clean, bright and airy facilities, respectable office space, and support people to perform those tasks that detract from teaching. Provision of such an atmosphere is an administrative responsibility that contributes much to making physical education a dignified teaching experience that generates pride in achievement due to responsible performance.

Conditions Specific to Program

For organizational development to occur successfully through process consultation, all participants must be willing to enter into joint, cooperative problem solving. The participants should agree that the quality of teaching needs to be improved.

Evaluation

There is no written evidence to indicate that this organizational development approach has been used to influence the quality of teaching in physical education. It has already been used extensively in business and industry with success. Other points worth noting include:

1. Changing nonteaching to teaching may cause massive internal conflict, regardless of the method of change.
2. Other forms of in-service programs (i.e., staff workshops) will not correct the problems of nonteaching when the problem is that teachers will not teach rather than that they cannot teach.
3. The organizational development process draws people together in problem-solving groups, with opportunities for input from all.
4. Improving the quality of teaching is a continuing process.
5. Using this approach may require the employment of outside consultants.
6. The process allows teachers to return to teaching without the threat of dismissal.
7. The cost to the school system and the administration for using this approach is the loss of absolute control and autonomy over the teachers.
8. The benefit for the school system is to gain good instructional programs.
9. Where change is desired, this approach can work; but nothing may be effective where resistance to change is high.

General Comments

The process of developing a school system that makes good teaching the rule rather than the exception is continuous. Teaching and learning are the primary goals of education. The organizational development process allows staff members to work toward good teaching and then develop strategies to ensure that good teaching continues.

For more complete information about organizational development, the reader may refer to:

Bobbitt, Jr., H., and others. *Organizational Behavior*. Englewood Cliffs, N.J.: Prentice-Hall, Inc., 1974.

Koontz, H., and C. O'Donnell. *Essentials of Management*. 2nd ed. New York: McGraw-Hill Book Company, 1978.

Schein, E. *Process Consultation*. Reading, Pa.: Addison-Wesley Publishing Company, 1969.

A Basketball Challenge

Submitted by: Marlowe Mullen

School: Greenwood Community
High School
615 Smith Valley Road
Greenwood, IN 46142

Summary

Physical education units should be a learning experience for every student. Because of availability of equipment and facilities, basketball is an activity that is often repeated time and time again throughout a student's physical education experience. Normally, fundamentals are stressed, some of the rules are taught, skills and written tests are given, and there is competition.

The greatest weakness in an approach of this type is that it gives little learning experience to the student who has competed on one or more of the school's basketball teams for two or three years. During the practice and testing of fundamentals, this student excels and at the same time is bored. During competition, this student dominates play for his team and as a result the student with little ability rarely touches the ball. Has either of them really been "taught" anything lasting about basketball?

The program described below has been effective for sophomore boys at Greenwood High School for several years.

Outline

1. Coaches are hired.
   A. Coach must be a member of the class.
   B. Coach must have experience in organized basketball (school team, preferably).
II. Coaches draft their teams.
   A. First draft choice goes to coach with least experience or lowest level of experience.
   B. Seven-man squads have been most effective.
III. Coaches have two weeks of practice time with their teams to teach them everything that is required and to practice any fundamentals that they deem necessary.
IV. A round-robin schedule is played, plus a double elimination tournament.
   A. Coaches are not allowed to compete for their teams.

V. Evaluations (skills and written) are completed during unit.

Description

Students with competitive experience are given new challenges in this unit. They must research or draw from memory and experience at least five different areas of knowledge. Each coach is required to teach his team:

1. One offensive play against a man-to-man defense, in addition to any options he wants to teach related to that play
2. One offensive play against a zone defense, in addition to any options he wants to teach related to that play
3. The man-to-man defense and the fundamentals that must be used while employing it (e.g., position in relation to man and basket, switching off, etc.)
4. Any zone defense and the movement patterns used with it
5. One special play other than another offensive play (e.g., fast break, full court press, out-of-bounds play under own basket, etc.)

In additional to being responsible for teaching these five items, coaches invariably find it necessary to work on traditional fundamentals, as well as some fundamentals with which many members of their teams are not familiar, such as blocking out for a rebound, setting picks, etc.

On the first day of practice, team members are given a blank set of diagram sheets by the instructor in order to copy their coach's five plays and defenses during this period. This "playbook" is collected and checked by the instructor at the end of the first period. If all playbooks for each team are diagrammed properly, then the playbooks are returned the next day and become the student's study notes for the written test as well as a personal playbook.

Beginning the second day of practice, each coach is responsible for a team. Each team is assigned to a basket (if facilities permit) and given the equipment desired (as long as equipment is available and divided equally among the teams). The coach is free to utilize the time in any way—calisthenics, warm-up drills, shooting drills, conditioning, or just working on the plays and fundamentals.

Each team member is responsible for learning each of the five plays taught by the coach. During the two weeks of practice sessions, the instructor should ask to see various plays and defenses, being sure to put substitutes in to check their progress also. Each student in this program is somewhat dependent on teammates, and in most cases this helps to foster teamwork and cooperation (especially for the slow learner). As grades on the skills test are partially dependent on everyone knowing the plays, team members are more tolerant and helpful with the less skilled students.

During the last three days of practice, scrimmage games are played. These games are refereed by the coaches and are used solely for the purpose of trying to utilize their plays against another team. During these scrimmages, the coaches are to stop the game whenever they wish to make any correction, no matter what is in progress. Scores are not kept during this training session.

The last phase of the basketball unit is competition. During competition, the coaches are restricted by the current high school basketball rules. (Some of the coaches come into the game carrying a clipboard and wearing a coat and tie.) If they are available from study hall or other free periods, the referees are varsity basketball players, who are instructed to make all calls according to the current high school rules (including calls against the benches).

Evaluations are made in the following manner:

1. Coaches are hired for the maximum amount of points available for what would normally be their skills test grade. Each time a coach is not doing the best job for his team, or if a coach is called for a technical violation during competition, a certain number of points are deducted from the coach's salary.

2. Players are evaluated by the instructor during competition. Each player is observed while playing and receives up to one-fifth of the grade on the skills test for each of the following items:

a. *Teamwork* (Does he cooperate with the coach and his teammates without complaint, and does he try to do what is best for his team without concern for personal goals?)

b. *Knowledge* (Does he demonstrate a mastery of the five diagrammed areas of knowledge for which he was responsible?)

c. *Defensive effort* (Does he give a total effort on defense at all times, no matter what the score of the game or what his defensive skill level is?)

d. *Sportsmanship* (Does he recognize the difference between competitiveness and unsportsmanlike behavior? Can he cope with "bad calls," team or personal failures, and personal fouls within the parameters of acceptable behavior?)

e. *Skills level* (Does he demonstrate a mastery of the fundamentals of basketball, i.e., passing, dribbling, and shooting?)

3. Written tests are given to all players and coaches. These consist of five blank diagram sheets on which each student must diagram the team's five learning objectives. These are graded by the coach (including his own) and then given to the instructor. If any item is marked correct by the coach but is not diagrammed correctly, then the coach's answer is wrong.

Conditions Specific to Program

This idea has been most successful when the following were included:

1. Facilities for each team to have its own basket during each practice session
2. After teams are selected, letting them choose a "team name" (invariably some of the names will have to be referred to by initial only)

3. If a team chooses to, allowing members to decorate their T-shirts with their team name and emblem (design to be approved by instructor)
4. Taking "team pictures" and posting them on the bulletin board, along with the team's roster and the season schedule and standings
5. Playing full court and using the basketball scoreboards during competition
6. Furnishing a whistle and a referee's shirt to knowledgeable referees
7. Being sure each coach uses everyone on the bench in every game
8. Setting up an after-school "play off" for the various class champions.

Evaluation

Strengths
1. A "learning situation" for everyone
2. An opportunity for everyone to play without being dominated by the best athletes in the class
3. Opportunity for experiencing the concepts of interdependence, teamwork, and cooperation in a way rarely provided in physical education
4. Insights for the "coaches" into the joys and frustrations of coaching, as well as forcing them to put their skills into words in order to "teach" instead of "do"

Weaknesses
1. There is always a potential for personality conflicts between players and coaches. If the coach is the only one who feels this conflict, then he must deal with it (just as all coaches do). If a player refuses to cooperate because of a conflict with the coach, that player may be traded (very early in the season) or put on waivers (keeping statistics or doing managerial work for the participation grade).
2. Adequate facilities are not always available.
3. The instructor does all of the evaluations (skills test scores) subjectively. Subjective grading can be opinionated and therefore biased.

Tennis,
Despite Weather
and Site Restrictions

Submitted by: Melinda Krumm

School: Benton Community Junior-Senior
High School
Van Horne, IA 52346

Summary

Because at times weather conditions do not permit use of the outside tennis courts, students are often required to hit tennis balls incessantly against gymnasium walls, where they gain little knowledge of how the game is actually played. When the students finally do get on the courts, the beginners spend most of their time chasing balls while many sit idly because of limited court space. Few experience the full routine of the game and therefore do not understand it. As many physical educators can attest, teaching students to keep score, serve, rotate properly, and execute a rally can itself be an exasperating experience without having to contend with logistical problems. However, these logistical problems plague many in their attempt to teach tennis.

To provide practical experience in the basics of tennis while learning the sequence of scoring, the game can be modified to enable it to be played off one wall while utilizing the ground space of a racquetball court. This allows two or four students to play a simulated game as well as to practice the skills of tennis. As a result, beginning students experience more success in hitting the ball against the wall than they would in trying to place it in a regulation tennis court. They can more readily master the scoring sequence and can concentrate on other aspects of the game. When they actually do get onto the courts, the chance that their first experience on the courts will be an overwhelming one will be lessened. Also, because of the success the students have had with the simulated game, they are not reluctant to return to it when conditions do not allow them to use the courts.

Outline

I. Practice of the basic strokes
II. Description of rules and scoring sequence
III. Performance of simulated games
IV. Evaluation of basic strokes, performance in simulated games, and knowledge of rules and scoring sequence

V. Review through practice and simulated games

Description

Diagram of Modified Court

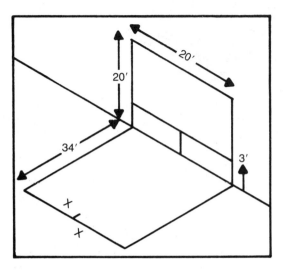

Sequence of Play
1. One student stands behind the baseline and on the right side of the center back line.
2. Another student stands behind or near the baseline on the left side of the center back line.
3. From behind the baseline, the student serves the ball, trying to hit it above the three-foot horizontal line on the wall and keep the ball below the top boundary line. The student may take two serves, if necessary.
4. The opponent attempts to return the serve.
5. The students alternate hitting the ball until one of them misses.
6. The server then steps to the other side of the baseline to serve again.
7. This rotation continues until the game is completed.
8. The opponent takes a turn at serving an entire game.

Conditions Specific to Idea

An important feature of the simulated game is that it is not restricted to a gymnasium setting. It allows for participation in almost any area that has enough wall space. For example, it can be played off the wall of a building in a parking lot.

Evaluation

Through the sequence of play the student has an opportunity to practice the following:
1. Correct scoring procedure
2. Proper rotation
3. Techniques of rallying
4. Basic strokes
5. Serve

Independent Learning Package of Basic Skills

Submitted by: Scott D. Kerby

School: California School for the Deaf
3044 Horace St.
Riverside, CA 92506

Summary

Independent learning packages covering four basic skill areas have been developed to further enhance skill development for students entering a secondary school physical education program. These allow the students to build a larger foundation of movement skills in preparation for a program with emphasis on more specialized skills and games and sports.

The four skill areas include ball handling, jump rope, balance, and stunts and tumbling. A task-complexity spectrum has been developed for each skill area, whereby the tasks are sequenced along a continuum in which they are increasingly more difficult to perform. Each skill area continuum has subsequently been divided to evolve three package levels of increasing difficulty.

Implementing independent learning packages early in the year is a strategy that teachers can use to assess skill development and identify students with special needs. The teacher is free to circulate about the class to encourage, motivate, and correct. This strategy also affords the underachiever some individual guidance from the teacher, while the more skilled students are not held back and can progress at their own rate.

The independent learning packages are unique in that they broaden the learning environment by integrating physical education activities with reading and comprehension, thus enhancing language development.

Outline

   I. Directions to the student
  II. Explanation of required activity
 III. Independent practice
 IV. Evaluation and teacher's initials

Description

Activity areas for each skill are set up with the necessary equipment and space. Each student is given a manila folder and a Level I package, as everyone begins with Level I. The students are encouraged to work with a partner of similar ability, although some tasks require more than two people. In a mainstream setting with hearing-impaired students, hearing students and hearing-impaired peers are required to work together to facilitate communication and social development. The class is then randomly divided among the four activity areas to begin work.

To achieve a task, the student must first read the direction and description of the task and then do appropriate practice. When the student feels that he or she has met the requirements of the task, the student's folder is presented to the teacher so the task can be initiated (indicating completion). The teacher may require a demonstration to assure proper performance. The students are rotated approximately every 10–15 minutes and work in two or three skill areas a day. The entire package level must be completed before passing on to a higher package level.

In Level II, for example, the student attempts 5–6 tasks each in ball handling, jump rope, balance, and stunts and tumbling. Jump rope tasks, with instructions to the student, are as follows:

1. With a large jump rope, run through without touching rope 5 times. *Things to look for:* Begin your move as rope hits the ground and run under the arch of the rope.
2. With a large jump rope, run through with a partner 5 times. *Things to look for:* Must go through together.
3. With a large jump rope, run in swinging rope, jump 25 times, then run out. *Things to look for:* Face one side or the other.
4. With a large jump rope, run in swinging rope with a partner, both of you jump 25 times, then run out together. *Things to look for:* Face your partner when jumping.
5. With a large jump rope, can 3 jumpers, all holding hands in a circle jump rope at the same time without letting go of hands for 10 jumps? Can all 3 jumpers move in a circular motion

without letting go of hands? *Things to look for:* Stay close together and keep your head up.
6. With a large jump rope and an individual jump rope, combine the two and try to jump both at the same time for 10 jumps. *Things to look for:* Try to keep ropes together, head up and feet together.

Conditions Specific to Program

A background of independent practice during a previous program is advantageous for successful implementation of independent learning packages. The student should have been given the opportunity to develop habits of creativity and discovery in order to become a self-motivated learner. Another prerequisite is that the student should understand the skills required and the vocabulary used in the packages.

Evaluation

Independent learning packages are an excellent device to assess the movement status of a class and allow the teacher to recognize characteristic problems that require attention and will need adjustment in future programs. The students progress at their own rate, while the teacher has the opportunity to assist those who need or desire help.

These packages are also an excellent tool to promote social development and communication between hearing and hearing-impaired students in a mainstream physical education setting. By working together, the two types of students learn how to communicate ideas, movements, and emotions through the various modes available to them.

It is often difficult to observe all the students, to initial their papers, and to help others unless assistants are available. Many times the more skilled students who finish ahead of the others may assist the teacher in a variety of ways.

Peer Teaching to Meet the Needs of Handicapped Students

Submitted by: Ed Long and Larry Irmer

School: Phoenix Union High School
District
2526 West Osborn Road
Phoenix, AZ 85017

Summary

Peer teaching is a concept and practice used in the Phoenix Union High School District to provide an individualized physical education program for handicapped students and others who have special needs. Peer tutors (student aides) are under the direct supervision of the teacher in a specially designed class called PEOPEL, which stands for Physical Education Opportunity Program for Exceptional-handicapped-Learners. PEOPEL's peer teaching is an alternative to, or an addition to, traditional adapted physical education where there are no student aides or peer tutors.

A PEOPEL class may have up to 30 students enrolled (15 handicapped students plus 15 peer tutors). Each PEOPEL student has a peer tutor for a partner for all activities. When students work and play together as partners, the teacher can more realistically provide an individualized program. Students must first complete an orientation class before they become peer tutors. The PEOPEL students are referred by special education teachers, counselors, and the school nurse.

The PEOPEL class is coeducational, fun, effective, and positive for students and peer tutors. Peer tutors receive physical education credit for participating in the orientation class and PEOPEL class.

Outline

I. Identify approximate number of students to be served by the program.
II. Identify enough student peer tutors so that each PEOPEL student will have a partner.
III. Orient and train student peer tutors regarding the class, their role as a peer tutor, and their responsibilities to students and teacher.
IV. Combine PEOPEL students and peer tutors to make the class(es).

Description

When a school decides that the use of student peer tutors in physical education for students who have special needs is a positive way to meet their individual needs, how does the school start a PEOPEL peer teaching class?

The program needs the cooperation and support of the administration, counselors, special education and physical education departments, and the school nurse. Students who would benefit are referred by the nurse and by physical education and special education personnel. Once the number of students has been established, the physical education department explains the class to potential student peer tutors. The teachers and counselors assist in identifying students who would be effective peer tutors in the PEOPEL class.

The physical education teacher "trains" the potential peer tutors before they begin their work and play with the handicapped students. This training may take two or more weeks, with the intent of familiarizing the peer tutor with the goals and objectives of the class, who the students are with whom they will be working, what are some motivational and counseling considerations, and what the roles and responsibilities of the peer tutor are. Student peer tutor training is outlined and described in a Student Aide Training Guide developed by the Phoenix Union High School District.

Once the peer tutors feel comfortable and confident about their role, the PEOPEL students and peer tutors are combined to form the PEOPEL class. In class, all students are under the direct supervision of the physical education teacher. Each student has a peer tutor partner for all activities. This partnership enables the teacher to more realistically provide for the individual needs of the handicapped students. The primary role of the peer tutor is to listen to the instructions given by the teacher and then provide positive feedback so that the student feels success in the activity. Peer tutors can measure the individual progress of PEOPEL students on performance objective charts that are contained and described in the PEOPEL Teacher's Guide developed by the Phoenix Union High School District. This guide contains 35 activity units, with student performance objectives explained for each activity.

Conditions Specific to Program

The PEOPEL Teacher's Guide and Student Aide Training Guide were written by physical education teachers in the Phoenix Union High School District. The PEOPEL program has achieved national validation by the U.S. Department of Education in Washington, D.C. As a nationally validated program, PEOPEL participates in awareness and staff training activities sponsored by the National Diffusion Network. A school that is interested in starting a PEOPEL program should contact the Phoenix Union High School District or the respective State Facilitator for the National Diffusion Network. The program and curriculum materials are provided to schools wishing to start a PEOPEL program. No specialized or expensive equipment is necessary to implement an effective PEOPEL class.

Evaluation

PEOPEL students are evaluated each year they are enrolled in the class. The evaluation includes a four-item physical fitness test, and a twenty-item reaction survey dealing with attitudes toward physical education and activity. Both evaluation components are administered on a pre-test and post-test basis. The strengths of a PEOPEL class are directly related to the following:

1. Administrative support for the class
2. Interdepartmental communication, cooperation, and support from counselors, special education and physical education teachers, and the school nurse
3. Interest and commitment by the PEOPEL teacher in training peer tutors and planning for the class
4. Interest and commitment by the peer tutors in receiving positive feedback from the successes of their partners.

General Comments

The concept and practice of using student peer tutors is a positive approach to meeting the needs of special students in physical education. In the Phoenix Union High School District (and more than a hundred other schools throughout North America), this class is called PEOPEL (Physical Education Opportunity Program for Exceptional-handicapped-Learners).

PEOPEL is not a commercial product. It is organized to make awareness and staff training presentations through the National Diffusion Network to schools wishing to start a program.

For additional information, contact Ed Long, Director, Physical Education and Athletics, or Larry Irmer, PEOPEL Coordinator, Phoenix Union High School District, 2526 West Osborn Rd., Phoenix, AZ 85017.

Let's Get Physical with Newspapers

Submitted by: Ann Schenk Junk

School: Sproul Junior High School
Security, CO 80911

Summary

Everyone needs a change—new ways to do the same old thing. The use of the newspaper in physical education classes can help. The intent is to help motivate and stimulate physical educators to use the newspaper in physical activities and provide activities in which students can be physical with the newspaper.

The tasks can be used either as a bonus opportunity or as make-up work when a student is injured or absent. If a student is absent on the skills day in basketball or the day the team plays volleyball for first place, using the newspaper for make-up work is appropriate. Students limited in physical ways greatly benefit from a physical activity that does not require some of the finer skills. The newspaper is easily used in an adaptive physical education class. The students are well informed of this opportunity to control their own future in physical education classes. Some students are natural athletes; the others need something to help them raise their self-confidence. The newspaper ideas provide many activities for students interested in bonus work to help improve the points earned in each unit.

Newspapers are provided daily through the physical education budget. A sheet called paperwork is printed and made available at the beginning of each sport unit, with a due date for full credit. Large motor skills are a must in physical education teaching philosophy, but for a break in routine teachers can try the newspaper ideas and then end the class with some of the physical ways to use the newspaper.

Outline

I. Written ways to use the newspaper in physical education
   A. Read, then do
   B. Read, then cut and paste
   C. Read, then draw or color
II. Picture ways to use the newspaper in physical education
   A. Collages
   B. Sport booklets
   C. Health booklets
III. Physical ways to use the newspaper in physical education

A. Exercising with the paper
B. Actual equipment substitutes

Description

Written Ways to Use the Newspaper

1. *Any sport bonus unit:* Find four pictures of officials giving a signal or call for a particular game or sport. What sport is it? What call is it? What do you have to do to become an official? Are there any officials among your teachers? Interview them. (25 points)

2. *Volleyball bonus unit:* Find three articles on volleyball. Write a report on what you read, listing:
   1. Ten names of volleyball people
   2. Five volleyball terms (example: right side attack)
   3. Two quotes from players or coaches
   4. Your opinion why volleyball is popular. (40 points)

3. *Any sport bonus unit:* Find an article that concerns a popular sports figure. Cut it out and attach it to the top of a piece of a paper, leaving room at the bottom. Find all the words that are unknown to you on first reading. Make a list of at least ten of these unknown vocabulary words. Look up the words in a dictionary, making sure the definition fits the article. (30 points)

4. *Names:* Go through the paper looking for teachers' names or the name of your school. Cut the articles out and glue on a piece of paper. (20 points)

5. *Words:* Take one sports section from the paper and cut out all the WINNING, WIN, WON words that you can find. Put these words in an envelope. On the outside of the envelope write one sentence why winning is important to you, and write one sentence why winning is not important to you. On the other side, list five synonyms for winning.

6. *Track bonus unit:* Cut out four pictures or articles concerning stretching. What sport is it used for? What muscles are being used? (List them for each picture.) What is your definition of stretching out? Name two stretching exercises done in class. (35 points)

7. *Gymnastics bonus unit:* Find three pictures or articles concerning gymnastics. Cut them out and staple them together, with a title page on the top. The title page should give the following information for each picture:
   1. Date when found
   2. Name of paper
   3. Outstanding point about the picture
   4. Student's name and class period
   5. One positive sentence about gymnastics

8. *Basketball bonus unit:* Collect pictures of basketball players with ten different uniforms on their body. Staple them together, with a page written out for identification of school or team that the player represents. (maximum 50 points)

9. *Football bonus unit:* Find advertisements in the newspaper for five different kinds of football shoes. Which ones would you buy? Why? Turn in all information. (30 points)

10. *Bicycling:* Find an article about bicycling in the newspaper. Draw a picture of a bicycle, naming the parts. Do you own a bicycle? Find two advertisements about a bicycle for sale. Which one is the better for your needs? (40 points)

11. *Calendar:* The calendar below shows the logos for the Nuggets, the Rockies, and the Avalanche teams. Draw them larger and color them as you please.

Picture Ways to Use the Newspaper

The teacher saves the best variety of posters, booklets, and drawings from the past year to put up (just to give some ideas). The first project of the year is to make a sports collage from the newspaper. If possible, have some paper (butcher paper, old construction paper, old posters, paper bags) on hand to encourage originality.

1. *Collages:* Ideas include pictures cut out in various shapes, titled or untitled, using different backings or detailed cutting, adding original drawings, and anything else the students might invent.

2. *Sport booklets:* These include diagrams of courts, history of the sport, pictures of

	MONDAY FEB.8	TUESDAY FEB.9	WEDNS. FEB.10	THURSDAY FEB.11	FRIDAY FEB.12	SATURDAY FEB.13	SUNDAY FEB.7
NUGGETS			UTAH 7:35 P.M.			SAN DIEGO 7:35 P.M.	WASH. 11:05 A.M.
ROCKIES					QUEBEC 7:35 P.M.		
AVALANCHE					BALTIMORE 5:35 P.M.		PHILA.

players, scores, etc. Students should decorate the front page artistically.

3. *Health and related subject booklets:* These stress family relations, drug and alcohol abuse, addictions, friendships, and other topics pertinent to the student's feelings. Again, it is suggested that they decorate the front cover to their liking.

Physical Ways to Use the Newspaper

1. Get a partner and a page of the paper. Each partner makes a tight ball with the paper. Pass the paper balls back and fourth, with under-the-leg pass, behind-the-back pass, and figure-eight pass between the legs. Thinking of all the skills in basketball, try to do those same skills with paper balls.

2. Using a section of the paper, roll it into a long tube (like a barbell), taping it so that it will not unfold. Do some stretching exercises with it; step over it; put it behind your back and lift it. Pretend that it weighs 50 pounds. How hard would it be to lift? Now pretend that it weighs 5 pounds. What is the difference? How much do you weigh? How much could you lift? Get a scale and weigh yourself and the paper tube.

3. Make up a game with three others in the class, using the newspaper as a piece of equipment. Demonstrate it and explain the rules.

4. Stand on one page of the paper. Can you pick it up to knee level with your toes? Can you hang on to it long enough to do ten leg lifts with it? Try both right and left legs. Do leg circles, too.

5. Place one page of the paper unfolded behind your back. Can you fold it in half? in fourths? in eighths? Wad it up into a tight ball and toss it back and forth over your head ten times without dropping it to the floor.

Conditions Specific to Idea

The teacher should:
1. Make sure the information is accessible. Put the information in the same place each time. Request they turn it in to the same spot also.
2. Make sure class is aware of the location of the newspapers.
3. Use newspaper pictures and articles for the bulletin board in the room.
4. Give key ideas on what to write about on your handout. You do not want the article reprinted.
5. Relate the reading or finding of the article to the sport unit being taught in class.
6. Add a cartoon or picture or drawing on the handout. Make it look fun to do.

Evaluation

If possible, show what the reward will be for completing the task on the paperwork. When working on a point basis, it becomes simple to assign points to the task. The completion of the task is the main objective, so a maximum number of points should be set for each task. Some students will naturally work harder and be more detailed and complete; therefore, the teacher should make it clear that there is a maximum number of points.

Experience has shown that these projects relate especially to all students who are willing to do something a little extra. They are effective when students have special needs. They should not be used to discipline a student. A very positive approach to using the newspaper in physical education is best.

General Comments

To maintain the valuable position of physical education in the school system, it becomes increasingly important to expand the program to the maximum. The newspaper and other printed materials in the physical education program are tools that keep the physical education program updated and vital to the overall educational process.

Contingency Contracts for Junior High School Physical Education

Submitted by: Dr. Paul W. Darst
Arizona State University
Ken Coyle
McKemy Junior High
School

Schools: McKemy Junior High School
2250 South College Ave.
Tempe, AZ 85281

Arizona State University
Dept. HPE, 128 PEW.
Tempe, AZ 85287

Summary

Contingency contracts have been developed and field-tested in a number of physical activity units at McKemy Junior High School. The units are usually three weeks long and meet five days a week. All classes are coeducational. The contracts have been introduced and used in a number of different ways. The activities include flag football, soccer, field hockey, volleyball, lacrosse, weight training, team handball, basketball, and badminton. The contracts have been found to be an excellent way of organizing a teaching-learning environ-ment because they enhance the motivation of both the teacher and the student.

Students at all levels of ability should be able to find success and a challenge in a properly constructed contingency contract. Students can progress through the learning tasks at their own rate, and teachers can provide increased rates of praise, feedback, and motivational cues in this teaching format. These contracts can be effective with various grade levels and various physical education activities.

Outline

The following is an example of a coeducational volleyball contract that has been used with seventh and eighth grade students:

I. Core Requirements
   Forearm Pass (Bump) Tasks
   _____ 1. Bump 6 consecutive forearm passes into the air to yourself at a height of at least 10 feet. (1 point)
   _____ 2. Bump 6 consecutive forearm passes over the net to a partner or with the instructor. (1 point)
   _____ 3. Bump 6 consecutive forearm passes against a wall at a height

of 6½ feet while standing behind a restraining line 4 feet from the wall. (1 point)

Overhead Set Pass Tasks

_____ 4. Hit 6 consecutive set passes into the air at a height of at least 10 feet. (1 point)

_____ 5. Hit 6 consecutive set passes over the net with a partner or with the instructor. (1 point)

_____ 6. Hit 6 consecutive set passes against a wall at a height of 6½ feet while standing behind a restraining line 4 feet from the wall. (1 point)

Serving Tasks

_____ 7. Hit 3 of 5 consecutive underhand serves into the right half of the court. (1 point)

_____ 8. Hit 3 of 5 consecutive underhand serves into the left half of the court. (1 point)

_____ 9. Hit 3 of 5 consecutive overhand serves into the right half of the court. (1 point)

_____ 10. Hit 3 of 5 consecutive overhand serves into the left half of the court. (1 point)

Dig Task

_____ 11. With a partner tossing the ball over the net, dig 3 consecutive underhand shots. (1 point)

Net Recovery Task

_____ 12. With a partner tossing the ball into the net, recover 3 consecutive balls. (1 point)

Attendance and Participation

_____ 13. Be ready to participate in volleyball activities 5 minutes after the last bell rings each day. (⅕ pt. daily = 1 pt. weekly)

_____ 14. Use proper locker room behavior (will be discussed and/or posted at all times). (⅕ pt. daily = 1 pt. weekly)

_____ 15. Score at least 80% on a written test (2 attempts only). (5 points)

  II. Optional Tasks

_____ 16. Volley 8 consecutive times over the net with a partner by alternating forearm (bump) passes and overhead passes. (2 points)

_____ 17. Recover a ball from the net (recoveries must be playable) during a game. (2 points)

_____ 18. Hit 3 of 5 overhead passes from the foul line that hit the basketball rim. (1 point)

_____ 19. Alternate forearm passes (bump) and overhead passes in the air at a height of 10 feet or more for 6 consecutive times. (3 points)

_____ 20. Standing in the server's position (right corner backline), bump 3 of 5 forearm passes into targets (hula loops) located near the net. (3 points)

_____ 21. Standing in the setter's position, hit 3 consecutive overhead sets at least 10 feet high that land inside a target (hula loop). The ball will be thrown by a partner. (2 points)

_____ 22. Hit 3 consecutive overhead serves into the right half of the court. (1 point)

_____ 23. Hit 3 consecutive underhand serves into the left half of the court. (1 point)

_____ 24. Diagram a volleyball court with all the dimensions and markings. (2 points)

_____ 25. Write up a list of 15 terms about volleyball and define them. (2 points)

_____ 26. Score the winning point for your team during a regulation game. (2 points)

_____ 27. Write a one-page report on the history of volleyball in the United States. (2 points)

_____ 28. Write a one-page report (summary) on Al Scate's book, *Winning Volleyball*. (3 points)

_____ 29. Officiate at least half of a volleyball game, using proper calls during class time. (1 point)

 III. Grading Structure

   18 points = C
   23 points = B
   28 points = A

The instructor reserves the right to lower these totals, if necessary, but will not raise these totals for any reason.

Description

The contracts are usually introduced in four stations set up to work on the contract tasks. The contracts are posted on a wall, a boundary cone, or a post for the net, with the specific objectives circled on the contract. The instructor takes the students as a group to each station and briefly explains and demonstrates the specifics of each task. Targets and balls are available at each station. Students then spend 1–5 minutes working on the tasks at each station. The teacher can control the amount of time spent at each station, depending on the ability of the class and the place in the unit. The teacher is free to move about and help students.

Students can be given a copy of the contract and encouraged to work on the tasks at home with their parents and friends. The stations and specific tasks can remain the same or be changed daily to ensure a challenge and success for all ability levels. Evaluation and recording procedures vary, depending on the teacher and the class. An effective procedure is to use a combination of teacher, student leaders, peers, and self-evaluation.

Conditions Specific to Program

A nice aspect of these contracts is that they can be adapted or modified to fit a particular situation. No special equipment is needed other than the basic equipment for the activity. Targets can be made out of boxes, jump ropes, boundary cones, tires, or other materials. Obviously, the contracts must be developed and duplicated for students.

Evaluation

The contingency contract, which specifies a relationship between a behavior and the consequences of that behavior, can be used as a motivational device and as a grading scheme. The model, which is based on the principles of psychology and the behavioral work of B.F. Skinner, offers a number of interesting advantages. The following are possibilities:

1. Students know what is expected of them.
2. Students seem highly motivated.
3. The contract format provides all students with some success as well as a challenge.
4. Students can progress at their own rate.
5. Students have some options for learning activities.
6. Students are forced to accept responsibility for learning.
7. The contract emphasizes learning rather than teaching.
8. Students can work together or individually.
9. The contract format can help to reduce in-class time spent on management or directions and can increase the time for teachers to spend as an agent of feedback.
10. Finally, the contract format enables administrators, supervisors, and parents to know exactly what is expected and what has been accomplished by the students.

Copies of the contracts and more specific information are available from the authors.

Reward Incentives

Submitted by: Dr. Sue Whiddon

School: University of Florida
Gainesville, FL 32611

Summary

In the Alachua and Marion County public schools, interns and teachers employ various easy-to-administer and inexpensive ideas for student recognition. Challenging incentives to promote active participation can reduce discipline problems and present an alternative to grades as a reward for outstanding performance and effort.

Outline

    I. Recognition clubs
    II. Skill charts
    III. Spotlight board
    IV. Awards

Description

Recognition Clubs

To complement tournament competition, students who attain a specific goal during class or intramural sessions should be recognized. For example, in teaching archery, a Bulls-eye Club could be established. Names of those who have achieved the status of belonging to the club by scoring a bulls-eye are displayed in the gymnasium, in the locker room, or on the physical education bulletin board. Additions to the display are posted daily.

Examples of the adaptability of this idea to other activities include a Par Club for golf, a 200-Game Club or Turkey Club in bowling, and a Dead Ringer Club in horseshoes. Certain activities, such as jogging and swimming, lend themselves to achievements in terms of accumulated distances. For example, a 100-Mile Club allows students to achieve this goal at their own pace or within a reasonable time period. Minimal records are kept to show daily progress. For added incentive, various levels of achievement may be designated by offering clubs named for various distances (100 or 200 miles, etc.). Again, upon accomplishment, the student's name is displayed in an appropriate location. Certificates or other symbols may or may not be desirable.

Skill Charts

Once skills are properly presented, each student needs time to practice and develop these through individual, reciprocal, or teacher-assisted work. Activities with multi-events, such as gymnastics and track and field, or those with multi-skills, are ideal for the employment of skill charts and station-to-station teaching. Using an individualized instructional approach, students progress at their own rate, with the instructor acting as a checking agent. On evaluation days, each student designates the skills which he or she wishes to attempt. The check sheets for every event may be kept on a clipboard or a bulletin board. Skills for each event are listed from lesser to greater difficulty (including performance time or distances, when appropriate). Most skills should be achievable with effort, for all. When ability grouping is used, charts incorporate appropriate skills for the various levels. Skill charts also assist the instructor in the evaluation process and allow students to calculate that portion of their own grade.

Spotlight Board

Photographs on a spotlight board provide an inexpensive yet effective tool to (1) recognize individuals or teams for winning or sportsmanlike performances, (2) designate team leaders, (3) demonstrate good skill technique by class members, or (4) identify those who participate or represent the class or school in a particular event. Students are attracted to newspaper clippings or bulletin boards displaying pictures of themselves or friends. Many will derive satisfaction from the special attention. Previous school record holders may also be mentioned.

Awards

Fort King Middle School offers the AAHPERD Health Related Fitness Test at the beginning and end of each school year. Since initiating the awards program, the physical educators have alleviated a problem commonly associated with the pre-test and post-test methods. To encourage maximum performance, T-shirts are awarded to those performing well on the first administration of the tests. Standard awards are given to those achieving scores in higher percentiles on the second test.

At the end of the year, trophies are awarded to the outstanding male and female students. Criteria for selection include participation effort, physical education improvement, and performance. Awards may be presented during an all-school assembly. To avoid trophy expenses, certificates may be given; or a stationary plaque containing name plates for each year's recipients could be placed in a showcase or visible location.

Conditions Specific to Idea

Awards may be donated from local fitness and athletic establishments or may be included in the annual equipment requisition. Photographs may be taken by a member of the school newspaper staff, a faculty member, or amateur photographer in the school for the cost of film and processing.

Evaluation

Strengths
1. Students have an opportunity to gain recognition and individual attention.
2. Materials can be inexpensive and homemade.

Weaknesses
1. Trophies, if desired, may be expensive.
2. Students of lesser abilities may not be challenged initially. When grouping for competition and formulating goals, the instructor should keep in mind the need of all students to succeed and be recognized for some achievement.

General Comments

Although students should participate in activity for the intrinsic values, simple extrinsic rewards may encourage better performance. With improvement in skills, an increase in interest is generally found.

Individualized Weight Training

Submitted by: Duane Buturusis
Anita Krieger
Lucas Palermo
Dawn Heller

School: Riverside-Brookfield Township
High School
First Avenue and Ridgewood Rd.
Riverside, IL 60546

Summary

Weight training has become an integral part of physical education curriculums and athletic programs. The facilities and equipment used in these programs are apparatus, usually of the multi-station type. The mode of educating customarily centers around the coach or instructor, who dictates the practice and prescription. After extensive study in the strengths and values of individualized instruction, the format of the weight training course at Riverside-Brookfield Township High School has changed from a teacher-centered course to one of individualized instruction. Books, manuals, posters, and file cards were previously used as teaching and resource materials, but the media resource needed a more dynamic delivery system for the individualized weight training course. For this reason, sound film loops were created to explain and illustrate the materials presented on the posters, in the books, on the instructional cards, and in the training manuals.

The delivery system was later upgraded by acquiring 16mm training films produced by weight training equipment companies. The latest innovation is the creation of instructional video tapes. The goal is to have an instructional tape for every station in the strength fitness facility. As a result, the facility is the most popular in the curriculum and the most efficient teaching station.

Outline

I. Student weight training assessment
II. Introduction to weight training
    A. Grading procedures
    B. History of the Strength Fitness Facility
    C. Weight training terminology
    D. Safety procedures associated with weight training
III. Beginning phase
    A. Three modules required

1. Isotonic exercise
2. Isokinetic exercise
3. Variable resistance exercise
B. Module requirements
   1. How to do each exercise (learn by)
   2. How to practice each exercise—refer to evaluation checklist (practice by)
   3. Test over materials—refer to evaluation checklist (prove by)
IV. Intermediate phase
A. One of three modules required
   1. Circuit weight training
   2. Isometric training
   3. Training for powerlifting
B. Module requirements
   1. How to do each exercise (learn by)
   2. How to practice each exercise—refer to evaluation checklist (practice by)
   3. Test over materials—refer to evaluation checklist (prove by)

Description

Weight training is offered on all four levels of the coeducational physical education curriculum. The following is what a student will experience from the first day until the fourth and last week of the course.

The students enrolled in the class assemble in an area where the instructor presents an overview of the course. Handouts are given to the students concerning grading procedures, the history of the Strength Fitness Facility, weight training terminology, and safety procedures in the weight room. Following this presentation, the students fill out their assessment forms (see below). From the answers the instructor can differentiate between the advanced and inexperienced lifters. At the second meeting of the class, each student receives an evaluation checklist which will serve as the guide to the course. A duplicate copy can be kept by the instructor to aid the instructor in measuring the student's progress and to serve as a final grade sheet.

The three groups in which students can be classified are beginner, intermediate, and advanced.

Beginning phase

The beginning lifter, whose level has been determined by the information on the assessment form, has little if any experience or understanding of most of the exercises and types of training. For the beginner, three basic training modules apply:

1. Isokinetics using Hydra Gym equipment
2. Isotonics using Universal Gym equipment
3. Variable resistance isotonics using Nautilis equipment.

Each module consists of a wide variety of media presentations ranging from printed materials, such as a poster detailing each module, weight training books, and photographic instructional cards, to sound motion pictures by different weight training companies and to instructional video tapes. The beginner must practice and demonstrate all of the lifts included in each of the training modules.

A beginning lifter will start with the introduction to weight training. Among other things, the student must pass a written exam covering handout information distributed to all of the students on the first day. When the beginning lifter completes all of the introduction module, the student may now select one of the beginning training modules (isokinetics, isotonics, or variable resistance) to begin his work.

Within each module there are four basic requirements for the beginner to complete:

1. Student reads the "learn by" section of the poster, which contains a basic explanation of the exercises for that particular training module through pictures and captions.
2. Student views the media presentations corresponding with that module as many times as necessary. From this presentation, a more detailed description of the tech-

niques required to perform each exercise is obtained.

3. Student reads the "practice by" section of the poster, which explains the number of repetitions the bar should be lifted, the duration of the lift, and the amount of resistance to be used to practice each exercise. For example, the student can practice the vertical butterfly while facing the mirrors, checking position in relationship to the demonstrations.

4. Once the student feels capable of executing all of the exercises in the module, the student reads the "prove by" section of the poster and is required to perform one or more of the exercises randomly selected by the instructor or student leader in order to gain credit. The instructor then records the results on the checklist.

Each module must be successfully completed before the student can advance to the next. Completion of all three modules of the beginning phase takes an average of two weeks per student.

Intermediate Phase

Once classified as an intermediate lifter, the student must complete the requirements outlined for the intermediate phase.

The intermediate phase begins a more specific individualized training program. The three training modules relative to this group are circuit weight training, isometric training, and powerlifting techniques. The format of these training modules is similar to that of the beginning modules.

Students placed in this group are required to select only one of the three modules. For example, a student who is interested in strength development and cardiovascular conditioning selects the circuit weight training module, using the Hydra Gym equipment. The student directs his attention to the corresponding poster and then reads the "learn by" section to determine what exercises are designated

for the circuit training. Next, the student refers to the "practice by" section, which gives the specifications of each of the circuits. The student can view a sound loop film or read a manual or poster, if necessary, to review any of the exercises. Finally, to gain credit, the student must read the "prove by" section of the poster and perform a circuit twice during one class period within the limits indicated.

Two other modules are available to the intermediate student: isometric training and powerlifting techniques. Further information and details on these modules as well as the advanced phase materials can be obtained by contacting the authors.

It is intended that a student take weight training at least two times during the four years. For students who are unable to participate in the activity but elect to remain in the class, an adjusted program has been designed. This program contains more theory than practice. In order for these students to obtain credit for the different training modules, an accompanying questionnaire must be completed. Sample questions might be: "While a fellow classmate performs the arm curl, what primary muscles do you notice in action? Do your observations correspond to the printed material?"

At the conclusion of the weight training class, each student is asked to fill out an opinionnaire. This serves as an aid to the instructor when assessing the strengths and weaknesses of the course.

Conditions Specific to Program

Modules are designed to utilize the equipment available and can be rewritten to accommodate any changes or additions. Books, posters, file cards, and commercially available 16mm films were the first resources used. The training manuals, sound film loops, and video tapes were written by the staff, performed by students, and produced in the audiovisual center.

Evaluation

1. Students appraise themselves and work at their own strength level.

2. Students make realistic goals from beginner to advanced phases and work at their own rate.

3. The teacher is available for individual help.

4. Programs can be designed to suit any situation, facility, or needs.

Weight Training Assessment

Name _____ Date _____ Period _____

DIRECTIONS: Please answer the questions below as accurately as possible. Your answers will be helpful to plan with you ways which will help you to learn weight training.

yes	some	no	question
			1. Have you ever weight trained before?
			where _____
			2. Have you ever had weight training instruction?
			when _____
			where _____
			3. Do you consider yourself to be strong?
			4. Do you consider yourself to be powerful?
			5. Do you consider yourself to be proportionately fit?
			what part(s) of your body are
			not _____
			6. Do you consider yourself to be aerobically fit?
			7. Are you looking forward to learning weight training?

comments: _____

AN OUTLINE OF THE COURSE CREDITS

Beginning Phase—all 4 modules below required

Introduction	Isotonic Exercise	Isokinetic Exercise	Variable Resistance Ex.
10 points credit— practical exam or written exam	5 points credit—upper body (1 × 8-12) or written exam 5 points credit—lower body (1 × 12-20) or written exam	5 points credit—H-1 to H-8 (1 × 12-20) or written exam 5 points credit—H-9 to H-16 (1 × 12-20) or written exam	5 points credit— Nautilus (1 × 8-12) or written exam 5 points credit— Universal (1 × 8-12) or written exam
(max. credit—10 points)	(max. credit—10 points)	(max. credit—10 points)	(max. credit—10 points)

Intermediate Phase—you must choose 1 of 3 modules below

Circuit Weight Training	Powerlifting Training	Isometric Training
10 points credit— (2 × Circuit A) or written exam 10 points credit— (2 × Circuit B) or written exam	10 points credit—each exercise (1 × 5–8) or written exam 10 points credit—each exercise (1 × 1 max.) or written exam	10 points credit—each exercise (1 × 8 sec.) or written exam 10 points credit—each exercise, different bar position (1 × 8 sec.) or written exam
(max. credit—20 points)	(max. credit—20 points)	(max. credit—20 points)

Advanced Phase—ultimate goal

Training for Personal Goals
establish personalized workout from information from previous experience
5 points credit—for each day you execute workout outlined on your Personalized Workout Form
(max. credit—60 points)

Evaluation Check List
Beginning Phase
(all 4 modules required)

Student _____ Date _____ Period _____

INTRODUCTION

Practice By: for topics listed below, follow this practice sequence

check off

grips—for each grip, select exercise, verbally identify grip used _____
key selector—locate station U-1, place key selector in 70 lb. slot of wt. stack _____
dial in resistance—locate station H-1, dial in heaviest resistance on cylinder _____
plateloading—locate station N-1, place 2×25 lb. plates on weight stems _____

Prove By: 10 points credit—practical exam or written exam   credit _____

(maximum credit—10 points)

ISOTONIC EXERCISE

Practice By: for each exercise, follow this practice sequence (1 × 12)

	U-1	U-4	U-4	U-9	U-14	U-14	U-20	U-6	U-16	U-8	U-19	U-5	U-10
resistance													
repetitions													

Prove By: 5 points credit—(1 × 8-12)   5 points credit—(1 × 12-20)

	U-1	U-9	U-20	U-6	U-19	U-5
resistance						
repetitions						

and

	U-4	U-4	U-14	U-14	U-16	U-8	U-10
resistance							
repetitions							

or take written exam   or take written exam

credit _____

(maximum credit—10 points)

ISOKINETIC EXERCISE

Practice By: for each exercise, follow this practice sequence (1 × 12)

	H-1	H-2	H-3	H-4	H-5	H-6	H-7	H-8	H-9	H-10	H-11	H-12	H-13	H-14	H-15	H-16	H-17
repetitions																	

Prove By: 5 points credit—(1 × 12-20)   5 points credit—(1 × 12-20)

	H-1	H-2	H-3	H-4	H-5	H-6	H-7	H-8
repetitions								

and

	H-9	H-10	H-11	H-12	H-13	H-14	H-15	H-16
repetitions								

or take written exam   or take written exam

credit _____

(maximum credit—10 points)

VARIABLE RESISTANCE EXERCISE

Practice By: for each exercise, follow this practice sequence (1 × 12)

	N-1	N-2	N-3	N-4	U-18	U-15	U-24	U-22	U-25
resistance									
repetitions									

Prove By: 5 points credit—(1 × 8-12)   5 points credit—(1 × 8-12)

	N-1	N-2	N-3	N-4
resistance				
repetitions				

and

	U-18	U-15	U-24	U-22	U-25
resistance					
repetitions					

or take written exam   or take written exam

credit _____

(maximum credit—10 points)

total _____

Evaluation Checklist
Intermediate Phase
(choose 1 of 3 modules)

Student _____ Date _____ Period _____

CIRCUIT WEIGHT TRAINING
Practice By: follow this practice sequence—Circuit A (1 × 20 seconds)

	H-1	H-7	H-13	H-3	H-16	H-4	H-6	H-5	H-14	H-9	H-15	H-10
repetitions												

Circuit B—upper body exercises (1 × 8-12), lower body exercises (1 × 12-20)

	U-15	U-18	U-20	U-24	U-22	U-25	U-19	U-8	U-6	U-16	U-5	U-23
resistance												
repetitions												

Prove By: 10 points credit—2 sets of Circuit A

	H-1	H-7	H-13	H-3	H-16	H-4	H-6	H-5	H-14	H-9	H-15	H-10
reps. set #1												
reps. set #2												

or take written exam
and
10 points credit—2 sets of Circuit B

	U-15	U-18	U-20	U-24	U-22	U-25	U-19	U-8	U-6	U-16	U-5	U-23
resistance												
reps. set #1												
reps. set #2												

or take written exam

credit _____

(maximum credit—20 points)

Circuit Weight Training

Learn by: Refer to list of exercises on chart below,

and/or

Look at charts entitled Universal or Hydra Gym posted on weight room walls,

and/or

View training films by Universal and Hydra Gym,

and/or

View circuit weight training sound film loops,

and/or

Read training manuals, books, articles, etc. available at weight room desk upon request,

and/or

See physical education leader and/or instructor.

Circuit A
Hydra Gym-isokinetic
  squat (H-1)
  bench press (H-7)
  leg press (H-13)
  shoulder press (H-3)
  unilateral knee (H-16)
  leg curl (H-4)
  leg extension (H-6)
  upright row (H-5)
  ad/ab hip (H-14)
  arm curl (H-9)
  runner (H-15)
  abdominal (H-10)

Circuit B
Universal-isotonic
  chest press (U-15)
  leg press (U-18)
  upright row (U-20)
  leg curl (U-24)
  shoulder press (U-22)
  leg extension (U-25)
  lat pulldown (U-19)
  back arches (U-8)
  bicep curl (U-6)
  incline sit-ups (U-16)
  tricep extensions (U-5)
  leg raises (U-23)

Practice by: For each of above listed exercises, follow this practice sequence:

Circuit A
1. Get partner who will time and record for you.
2. Set dial (if necessary).
3. Assume starting position.
4. Respond to your partner's command to begin.
5. Push or lift bar as many times as possible for 20 seconds.
6. When your partner says stop, he should record number of complete repetitions performed during 20-second period.
7. Complete entire training circuit with 40-second rest between stations.

Circuit B
1. Get partner who will record for you.
2. Select weight to be used (if necessary) (60–70% of your maximum level).
3. Assume starting position.
4. Perform 1 set of 8–12 repetitions for upper body exercises and 12–20 repetitions for lower body exercises.
5. Your partner should record amount of resistance used and number of repetitions done.
6. Complete entire training circuit without rest between repetitions and stations.

Prove by: For 10 points credit:
     Do 2 sets of Circuit A in one class period
or
     Take written exam of 10 questions.
For 10 points credit:
     Do 2 sets of Circuit B in one class period,or
     Take written exam of 10 questions.
Refer to evaluation checklist first for more specific instructions.
Have physical education leader or instructor verify your work and record value on your Evaluation Checklist.
(maximum credit—20 points)

The SURE
Golf Swing

Submitted by: Jim Ewers
University of Utah
V. Farrell Thomas
Wasatch Junior High
School

School: Wasatch Junior High School
Salt Lake City, UT 84112

Summary

The golf swing is one of the most difficult motor skills to teach because the movement is so foreign to the natural fundamental skills that have been a part of most children's experience. The purposes of this unit are to offer (1) a concise description of the basic movement concepts in the golf swing, (2) drills, exercises, and teaching cues that can be used to develop the swing, (3) ideas to keep junior and senior high school students motivated to learn the golf swing, and (4) innovations for teaching golf on a playfield (soccer field, football field, playground, etc.).

Outline

I. Objectives
II. The four basic concepts of the full swing
III. The full swing through drills and practice
IV. Assessment of progress

Description

Specific objectives of a golf unit comprising 10–12 instructional classes devoted to the golf swing should be as follows:
1. Ability to hit the golf ball in the air in the direction of the target
2. Feeling of satisfaction and enjoyment in learning the golf swing
3. Understanding the causes for some of the basic errors in the golf swing
4. Development of patience as a learner

Teaching of the golf swing requires an understanding of the four basic concepts of the swing and how these can best be taught. The four concepts (1) Stretch, (2) Under, (3) Release, and (4) Extension are described as the SURE swing.

Basic to a good golf swing are preswing preparations, including a light and proper grip, a natural stance, and a comfortable set-up.

1. *Stretch*
   It is essential to keep the arms at full stretch throughout the swing—through

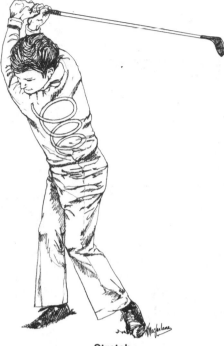

Stretch

Under

the backswing, the downswing, and the follow-through. A smooth one-piece take-away with a full coiling motion taken inside the target line is initiated by the left side. The key is to take the club back low and slow with the weight on the right side (back to target). Head and upper body are behind the ball, the left arm is extended and the right arm folds under to the side, passively relaxed but instantly ready to strike.

Swing sensation: Fully coiled extension, with springlike tension at the top of the swing.

2. *Under*

Arnold Palmer stated that the greatest feeling in golf is to stay under and follow through with the right shoulder low.

The first task before starting down is to complete the backswing. A slight pause at the top assures good rhythm and a smooth transition. The key is to start down in a leisurely and unhurried manner from a square position at the top (left hand, wrist, and forearm forming a straight line—no cupping, concaving, or

convexing). The left arm returns fully extended, using a pulling motion; left side leads the club into the hitting area and the right arm remains intimately close to side ready to release. The right shoulder moves down and under.

Swing sensation: The club is pulled down and through, maintaining that "coiled spring" as long as possible in the swing.

3. *Release*

The student is told to remember that the ball is incidental in the swing and it just happens to get in the way of a good release.

By taking a wider arc with full extension, the golfer is able to retain the angle of the club and the arms much longer and is able to reserve that precious club head speed until the precise moment of impact. This minimizes the role of the right side and maximizes the influence of the left side in pulling through the ball.

The right hand rolls over the left hand after impact in a forearm rotation sensation. The true test is not allowing the

Release

Extension

left hand and wrist to break down, collapse, buckle, or cup before and after impact. The key is to wait for the pull and then "let 'er rip," as the pros would say.

Swing sensation: A natural rotation of the forearms during the downswing.

4. *Extension*

Bobby Jones stated that the appearance of the player at the end of the effort will betray inconsistencies or confirm perfection.

The weight is on the outside of the left foot and toe of the right, abdomen and knees to target. Hands finish high and follow through with full extension. Head remains behind the plane where the ball was sitting at the address position.

Swing sensation: Extension to the end with the head back.

5. *Drills and exercises*

The following drills, with instructions to the student, are useful in teaching the golf swing:

a. *Low take-away drill:* From an address position, place a ball behind the club. As you take the club back into the stretch (backswing) position, keep the club low to the ground by turning the left shoulder, thus forcing

the club to roll the ball back at least 12 inches. This forces a good body turn.

b. *Body turn drill:* Place club behind your back holding club in the crease of your elbows. Turn your shoulders until club is pointing directly at the ball. Your back will point to the target with about 90% of your weight on your back foot. Start your downswing by shifting your weight to your front foot, rotating your sholders until the opposite end of the club is pointing to the ball. Your abdomen is now facing the target.

c. *Swish drill:* Turn club upside down and grip the shaft just below the club head with your left hand only. Take a normal address position, swing the club with your left arm and making the club "swish" as it moves through the impact area. This drill forces the transfer of weight from the back foot to the front foot.

d. *Mirror drill:* Execute the stretch (backswing) position in front of a full-length mirror (at home). Important check points are: (1) weight over back foot, (2) back knee over or slightly inside back foot, (3) left arm extended, and (4) back of left hand, no concaving, or no convexing.

   e. *3 o'clock drill:* Take the club back in your backswing to a position where the left arm is parallel to the ground (a 3 o'clock position). The club head should be pointing directly upward. From this position initiate the downswing with emphasis on the rotation of the forearms. Complete the swing when the right arm is parallel to the ground. Look for the three fingers on your left hand. Your left palm is facing directly upward. Begin this drill without hitting balls. As you develop consistency, begin hitting balls with this drill.

   f. *Right-hand off:* Take your backswing with both hands on the club. Begin the downswing with both hands on the club. As your hands approach the "hitting area," let go with your right hand and continue pulling through the ball with your left hand only. Be sure to pull through to the extension position. This drill permits the left side to pace the swing and helps keep your head behind the ball.

Conditions Specific to Program

The equipment needed to teach the golf swing, utilizing the above drills and exercises, consists of:

1. Golf clubs: preferably a short iron for each student, but at least one club for two students
2. Golf balls: some regular range balls and some whiffle balls
3. Wooden blocks with numbers painted on them from 1 to 9 to serve as tee markers
4. Target poles, such as ski poles or dowel rods approximately 4 feet long
5. Cloth to use for flags
6. Approximately 90 feet of clothesline rope, jump ropes, and round plastic hoops

7. Some token prizes and special awards, such as plaques or certificates
8. Score cards (3 × 5 inches) and pencils

A playfield approximately the size of a football or soccer field would be excellent for teaching golf, but a smaller space is adequate. Instructional resources of all types are available from the National Golf Foundation, 200 Castlewood Drive, North Palm Beach, Florida 33408. These resources include films, pictures, posters, instructional guides, and consultant services. There are hundreds of excellent golf films available. Some of these are designed and produced for instructional purposes while others are primarily entertainment. These are very good to be used in inclement weather.

Evaluation

Although there are several validated skill tests to assess golf performance, the most efficient and most effective way to evaluate the golf swing in a class situation is by observation or, even better, by video analysis. Evaluation by observation takes experience and study to be able to recognize a total performance that takes only a few seconds to execute.

In evaluating the golf swing, the following system meets some of the criteria for a good assessment technique. The points for each skill component are entered on a score card, with 25 points the maximum score.

Skill Components

1. *Address* (set-up) position includes grip, stance, body weight, body position, and alignment (1–5 points).
2. *Stretch* (backswing) position includes club take-away, body turn, body weight, arm positions, and club position at the top (1–5 points).
3. *Downswing* includes weight shift, club path, forearm release, head position, and extension (1–10 points).
4. *Performance* (1–5 points)
   Did the ball get airborne?
   Did the ball go straight?
   Did the ball go toward the target?
   Did the swing produce appropriate distance?

General Comments

Some ideas that have been effective in stimulating student interest in golf and making golf fun are presented below.

Contests with Prizes

It is advisable to have one contest during each class period, if possible. Some contests may merit a special prize (e.g., low score for the day or closest to the pin) while other contests may merely merit recognition without any tangible prize. The most cherished and appreciated prizes are simple, handcrafted plaques or trophies. In addition, bubble gum, individually wrapped candies, and golf balls (old and new) are well received.

1. Closest to pin contests, in which distances may vary according to the students' abilities and the space available
2. Long driving contests, using whiffle balls, using tennis balls, and using regular balls if space permits
3. Lowest score on the mini golf course set up on a playfield
4. Hitting the most shots in the fairway (an area designated as fairway about 20–30 yards wide, depending on the ability of the students)
5. Hitting the most shots over the football goal posts, baseball backstops, or pole vault standards from a designated area.

Video Equipment

Most schools have video equipment. Videotaping the golf swing is one of the best teaching techniques and provides excellent feedback to students. Although most students express dissatisfaction before being filmed, they cannot wait to watch themselves in action.

Mini Golf Course on Football Field

Using wooden blocks as tee markers and ski poles with flags and various size ropes or plastic hoops to make greens, a mini (9-hole) golf course may be laid out. Hazards (imaginary or real) may be added to make the course more difficult. Holes may vary in length from 20 yards to 40 yards, depending upon the space available. The course may be played with whiffle balls or regular golf balls.

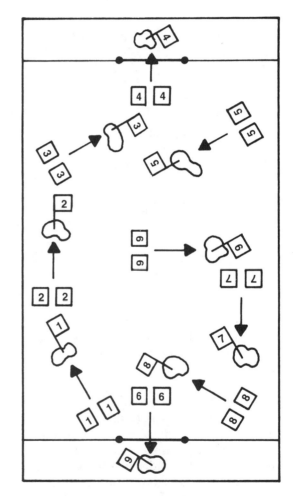

Mini golf course on playfield

A Bowling Program in the Gymnasium

Submitted by: Linda S. Fairman and
David Nitchman

School: Sheffield Middle School
1919 Harris Road
Lorain, OH 44054

Summary

A unique and innovative approach to bowling is being offered to students at Sheffield Middle School. The entire program, including the actual bowling, takes place in the school gymnasium.

As an alternative to taking physical education classes to the local bowling lanes, which proves costly and almost impossible with class scheduling, physical education teacher David Nitchman brought the bowling lanes to the students. Mr. Nitchman designed and built a complete, portable, eight-lane bowling alley for use in the school gymnasium.

Student enthusiasm, community support, and organization have all contributed to the success of this bowling program. Donations of bowling pins and balls by the local bowling establishments resulted in a two-lane expansion of the bowling lanes.

Outline

I. Scorekeeping
II. Ball selection
III. Three-step and four-step approaches
IV. Bowling etiquette
V. Test
VI. Bowling

Description

Each lane is regulation length and width, with masking tape indicating the gutter areas on either side. The first eight feet of each lane are covered by a ¼-inch thick piece of plywood which receives the initial impact of the ball on delivery and eliminates damage to the gymnasium floor.

A wooden ball-return on one side and 2-inch by 4-foot wood pieces nailed together on the other side divide each lane and keep the ball from rolling into another lane. To keep the ball from hitting the wall after it has knocked down the pins, a 6-foot wide folding tumbling mat is placed against the wall and on the floor behind the pins.

Plywood is used to receive the impact of the bowling ball, thus eliminating damage to the gymnasium floor.

Tumbling mats are placed against the wall and on the floor behind the pins. Triangular area is the safety area for pinsetters.

In order to keep flying pins from landing on another lane and as a safety measure for the pinsetter, wooden dividers 8 feet long by 32 inches high separate each lane next to the pins. The dividers are secured in place by hooks attached to the wall and a piece of plywood clamped across the top.

Every two lanes share a wooden ball-return trough that attaches to the wooden divider next to the pins. Placed at an incline, the trough connects to a return lane trough that proceeds down the alley and

ends at the ball-return rack. The ball is placed at the top of the incline and, when released, will travel down the trough and alley, up a small wooden incline and onto the ball rack.

Because students are used as pinsetters, a certain safety area is designated for students. Four triangular safety areas are used, with two students sharing each area. These triangles are located to the side and in front of the pin area. The pinsetter must be standing in this area before the bowler may

Every two lanes share a wooden ball-return trough that is attached to the wooden divider next to the pins.

Pinsetters must be standing in the triangular safety area before the bowler may bowl.

bowl. To aid the pinsetters, pre-measured spots placed on the floor indicate exactly where the pins should be set up.

Conditions Specific to Program

Much thought and planning went into the construction of the bowling alley. Because the gymnasium is used both before and after school for activities, one of the criteria in design and construction had to be portability. The lanes would be set up in the morning before classes and taken apart immediately after school.

Other considerations in construction included: (1) how to reduce the impact of a bowling ball on the gym floor; (2) how to keep a moving bowling ball on a lane, since actual gutters are not possible; (3) how to stop the bowling ball without damaging the walls, people, etc., after knocking down the pins; (4) how to keep flying pins in a restricted area; (5) how to reset the pins and return the ball back to the bowler quickly. All of these problems were solved with a little common sense, experimentation, a lot of plywood and lumber, and eight gymnasium mats.

Evaluation

Strengths
1. Students participate in a complete bowling program, including the actual bowling, right in their own gymnasium.
2. There are no game costs or rental fees.
3. Students share responsibilities; new scorekeepers and pinsetters are selected in each class.
4. Community awareness and involvement are obtained through donations of bowling balls, pins, etc.

Weaknesses
1. Setting up and taking down the lanes requires time and organization.
2. The completion of a regulation 10-frame game depends on the number of students in the class and length of the class period.
3. Wear and tear on the materials is only natural, and replacement of some of the lumber annually is essential.

Unit Grading for Junior High School Students

Submitted by: Terry Henage
Janice Douglas

School: Mexico Junior High School
1200 West Boulevard
Mexico, MO 65265

Summary

A unit grading system for junior high students has been developed and used. The grading system is designed to measure each student's achievement level during each physical activity unit. To justify every grade with valid and reliable data, four instruments are used to assess student learning. It has been found that this method of unit grading gives students maximum feedback of their achievement level, provides a system that students understand, and motivates students to learn all unit instructional concepts.

Outline

The unit grading system is comprised of four testing instruments:

I. Assessment of student's specific skill ability
II. Written test of knowledge
III. Subjective rating of student's class participation and performance
IV. Summative evaluation of physical fitness assignments

Description

Each unit carries an equal weight of 100 points. Because the instructional objectives are different for grades 6, 7, and 8, the point values of each measuring item are sometimes unequal:

	Grade 6	Grade 7	Grade 8
1. A test of student's ability to perform a specific skill	25	25	25
2. A written test of knowledge	25	30	35
3. A subjective rating of class participation and performance	25	20	15
4. Physical fitness assignments	25	25	25
	100	100	100

There are 100 points possible for each unit. Absolute grades are calculated by using the highest grade achieved by a student of the specific grade level and multiplying this total by absolute standards to find ranges for students' grades. A plus or minus is assigned if a student's point total falls on the bordering score of the ranges.

1. The highest score earned down 10% equals the letter grade of A.
2. The highest score earned down 11–20% equals the letter grade of B.
3. The highest score earned down 21–30% equals the letter grade of C.
4. The highest score earned down 31–40% equals the letter grade of D.
5. All scores below 40% equal a failing grade for the unit.

Unit Skill Tests

A skill test for each unit was developed and modified to validly, reliably, and objectively evaluate the student's skill level. Besides being a means of grading, skill tests also have proved to be a method of measurement of the attainment of unit objectives.

After each student's raw score is attained, it is converted to skill test points by the use of a conversion table. The sample below indicates the conversion of raw scores for archery into skill test points:

fx	Raw Score Ranges	Skill Test Points	Grade
5	135–116	25	A
9	115–100	24	A
14	99–91	23	A–
11	90–81	22	B+
12	80–72	21	B
18	71–61	20	B–
28	60–46	19	C+
52	45–31	18	C
18	30–22	17	C–
21	21–11	16	D+
8	10–0	15	D

cfx = 196

The procedure for developing the skill test conversion scale follows the rank-order method. Rank-order is an easy norm-referenced method of grading. First, a frequency distribution is constructed of all raw scores for that grade level. For the entire eighth grade class of 196 students, the upper 15% of the raw scores equal the A range. The next 20% of raw scores equal the B range. The next 50% of raw scores equal the C range, and the lower 15% are the D range. The number of skill test points is then assigned to the ranges. A standard percentage scale is assigned to the skill test points: A range would include 25–23 points, B range would include 22–20 points, C range would include 19–17 points, and the D range would include 16–15 points. No student can fail a skill test unless no effort is made to attempt the test.

With a large sample each year, the conversion scale can be revised and used annually.

Written Tests

The cognitive objective is measured by a written exam. Questions are objective in nature and review such unit knowledge as fitness values of the activity, physical skills required, knowledge of movement, strategy and rules of play, safety considerations and important terminology.

Subjective Rating

Although this item of evaluation has less weight and is subjective, it is vital to include in grading. The checklist below explains the factors considered in measuring class participation and performance:

Performance
_____ Team play
_____ Aggressiveness
_____ Strategy
_____ Demonstration of proper techniques and rules

Participation
_____ Promptness
_____ Classroom behavior
_____ Proper uniform
_____ Health habits
_____ Leadership
_____ Sportsmanship

Physical Fitness Assignments

Students are given an assignment at the beginning of class which gives them choices of cardiovascular fitness tasks. Students select the fitness task that is challenging and within their capabilities. The fitness assignments, when successfully completed, earn unit points and help develop the cardiovascular fitness level. The fitness tasks are progressive to ensure success for all ability levels. An example of a cardiovascular assignment is an activity called point trails. Students have three trails to select from: (1) a 650-yard trail that must be traveled in 4 minutes or less, which is worth 5 points if successfully completed, (2) a 550-yard trail that must be traveled in 3 minutes 30 seconds or less, which is worth 4 points, and (3) a 400-yard trail worth 3 points to be completed in 3 minutes or less. If a trail is not successfully completed in the time limit, 2 points are earned for the effort.

The fitness assignments are objective ways of measuring student effort and achievement. Some assignments carry less point value than point trails. Unit planning can ensure that 25 points are possible from fitness assignments at the end of the unit.

When all four measurements of student achievement are complete, the summation of the four scores indicate a student's point total and grade. Scores are posted at the end of each unit to provide immediate feedback to students.

Conditions Specific to Program

1. Unit instructional concepts determine the grading system to be used.
2. Enough unit activity days must be allowed so as to not use too much class time for testing.
3. This grading system is appropriate for coeducational classes.
4. The method of skill test conversion points is valid if a teacher's standards

are realistic in regard to the abilities of the students.
5. Weight of each testing instrument must be accurate for the evaluation desired.

Evaluation

Strengths
1. The unit grading system provides a comprehensive method of determining a student's grade.
2. Grades received are understandable and visible to the students.
3. A large portion of the unit grade is measured objectively.
4. Motivation to achieve is present for all class learning experiences.
5. Unit grading works for large and small classes, especially for coeducational classes.
6. Skill test conversion scales can be readjusted annually to validate the norms.
7. Students are placed in a responsible role to achieve and earn their grade.

Weaknesses
1. Initial use of this grading system requires time to develop measuring tools.
2. Units must be taught long enough to teach activity skills, present cognitive information, and actually play the activities. Too much testing can lessen the fun of play.
3. Selecting appropriate skill tests and establishing norm standards that are valid and reliable for coeducational classes requires practical judgment and knowledge of evaluation.
4. The subjective rating of performance and participation could be invalid if the teacher cannot measure each student's accomplishment.

Discipline, Choosing Teams, Square Dance, and Rope Skipping

Submitted by: Jim Brandon

School: Laredo Middle School
5000 S. Laredo St.
Aurora, CO 80015

Summary

The ideas presented here are intended to stimulate the reader toward rethinking and re-evaluating the areas of (1) discipline, (2) choosing teams, (3) square dance, and (4) rope skipping.

Discipline

Teachers cannot expect to manage a student's behavior, but they can manage their own reactions to situations and behaviors and try to set up an environment in which problems can be quickly and effectively dealt with as they occur. In order to accomplish this goal, teachers need some sort of systematic approach. First, it is necessary to identify behaviors that require disciplinary action and those that do not. Disciplinary action need not be taken except for the following: (1) behavior that interferes with efficient classroom operation, including other students' right to learn; (2) behavior that endangers the health and safety of students; and (3) behavior that may cause damage to student or school property. Students need to know and understand such guidelines. A policy handout sheet including these and any other specific rules is helpful in making students responsible for their actions and will clear up any miscommunication that may occur later. A commitment to enforce the rules must be made on a department-wide basis.

In spite of planning and organization, behavior problems will still exist. The key is that the student is responsible for his actions and that the disruptive student, not the teacher, has a problem. When a student is disruptive, care should be taken to give the student a graceful way out of the situation. Students need choices. One choice should always be simply to behave as a normal student should be behaving; the other choices dictate some sort of disciplinary action, such as doing a task or a short detention, or even more serious consequences for not complying. When this method is thoughtfully employed, the student can understand that the instructor is forced to act on the basis of student behavior and that the student is responsible for the consequences of his own actions. Discipline applied in this manner can become more objective for the teacher and student.

In order to keep the discipline system running smoothly, two concepts may be useful: (1) peer pressure, and (2) consistency. Peer pressure refers to the fact that the majority of students are anxious to do the lesson as planned and will help to control people who interfere with their opportunity for activity. Consistency means that the instructor does exactly what he says he would do and makes no idle threats. It is always necessary to follow up, so that there are no surprises and no comments about favoritism or picking on students.

Finally, some thought should be given to consequences for student behavior that does not meet the criteria. Although physical punishment (pushups, running laps, etc.) works to some extent, more problems result. Alternative measures are called for if the relationship between students and teacher is to be conducive to a better learning environment, a building of mutual trust and respect, and a classroom in which discipline problems seldom occur and can be dealt with quickly and effectively. Some measures that may meet these objectives are: (1) making students sit out of an activity; (2) short detentions; (3) seeing a student after class; (4) having the student make up the activity on his own time; (5) having the student write a short report on an appropriate subject; or (6) having the student help the department on his own time. All of these measures make the student responsible and do not put the teacher in a negative position. Students begin in a short time to understand the relationship between what they do and what happens to them as a result, and most of the time they learn to manage their behavior better. This eventually has a positive impact on the teacher's ability to be an effective instructor.

There will always be students who defy all attempts at being humanistic, and hopefully there is help at the school for dealing with these special problems. But day-to-day discipline can be managed effectively with careful thought, planning, consistency, a sense of humor, and common human decency.

Choosing Teams

One of the problems physical educators are faced with is coming up with reliable and efficient methods of forming teams for various activities. Organization by teams is instrumental in efficient classroom operation in a number of areas, but far more important goals can be explored in using teams. These include opportunities for meaningful social interaction, group loyalties, and teamwork toward common goals. Winning is not listed here as a prime goal. Working together toward doing the best one can, as a member of a group, is much more satisfying and important than just winning. Students work better when they are on teams or in groups of their own choosing rather than on teams or in groups that someone chose for them. The following method of choosing teams has been in use at Laredo Middle School for about four years. It is a combination of some commonly used methods and seems to be humanistic as well as efficient.

1. The instructor determines in advance the number of teams needed.
2. The instructor chooses a number of captains (one per team and only if team balance is required). This provides some positive recognition if the instructor splits the talent.
3. The class is told what the criteria are for a team (e.g., "Each team needs between six and eight people and at least two boys and two girls.").
4. Each captain should be given a few choices, but more than half of the class should not be chosen. The idea of choosing a few students for each team gives the captains someone to identify with, gives more students some positive recognition, and helps to provide some team balance. If six

teams are needed, captains should choose in this order to balance groups:

Team 1 has 1st and 12th choice.
Team 2 has 2nd and 11th choice.
Team 3 has 3rd and 10th choice.
Team 4 has 4th and 9th choice.
Team 5 has 5th and 8th choice.
Team 6 has 6th and 7th choice.

No matter how many choices per team are allowed, at least half of the class should be left to decide which team to join.

5. The criteria for teams should be repeated before giving the remaining students two or three minutes to get on a team (they do not all race to get on the same team because there are two, three, or four people per team to whom they relate). Instead of anyone having to be last, each student may now go to a team of first, second, or third choice (but the student's own choice). Most students are more willing to work when they are with a few friends. To those students who are reluctant to join a team, the instructor says something such as: "That team only has five people and could use you." Complaints from students already on a team are minimized because they are with at least some of their friends.

6. A spot check must be made to see whether the teams meet the criteria. If they do not, then adjustments can be made by asking for volunteers (preferably in friendly pairs) to switch teams or trade places.

7. Steps two and four may be omitted if team balance is not necessary.

Teams should now consist of groups of students who are willing to give each other support and who will work together to progress on skills for the benefit of the group as well as for themselves. Once a class becomes accustomed to this method, teams will be selected more quickly and with fewer problems than under the traditional methods of making teams.

Square Dance

Reasons abound for not teaching square dance in middle schools: they won't do it; they are too immature; they won't go near each other at that age; and square dance is too corny. At Laredo Middle School, square dance is taught, learned, and enjoyed. It must be admitted, however, that there are two basic problems. The first problem is to find another department member willing to teach dance. A man and a woman together have a much greater student motivational appeal than either one alone. This solved (and it may not be easy), there is the second problem—successful motivation.

Students have many of the same negative ideas that prevent instructors from teaching dance. A realistic alternative to behavior modification is needed. One such alternative is called forced compliance. It works like this. Students are encouarged to dance (techniques to be described). They find out that it is fun and that everybody else is doing it (eliminating embarrassment). When their behavior has changed, attitudes will change as a result of experiencing the activity. Knowledge will be forthcoming as the result of the desire to perform better. This system, along with the teacher's enthusiasm and motivational discussion, works better than just trying to talk students into acceptance.

To force compliance, the teacher acts as if he or she has been teaching dance for twenty years and that dancing in class is a normal expectation, not much different from football or basketball. It is important to get students dancing during the first session and to announce a skills test for the second or third session (and to really give it). Students should see the enthusiasm of both the man and woman who are teaching. It is important for the teachers to practice together so that demonstrations are good.

Music should not be too corny, if possible. A good sound system is essential and should be tested at the actual teaching station. The instructor must be familiar enough with the sound system to solve problems as they arise during class. A microphone should be used for large classes, especially when the teacher is doing the calling.

Classes are told before doing any dancing that boys' partners will not be boys and that two girls will not be partners. The teachers do not determine who dances with whom. They tell classes that a set (square) consists of at least four boys and four girls, and not more than eight boys or eight girls, before forming sets. The students get into their own groups. This helps eliminate fears of dancing with someone a student does not like. The teacher reminds the students a few times during this process that if they cannot make a decision, the teacher will be happy to help to make one. It is important to emphasize the set—not couples. Each set can be tested twice per evaluation, once through and then again with substitutes, so that everybody feels important in the group and knows that each student's contribution will be appreciated. Each member of the group gets whatever average score the set earns (with exceptions for individuals who stand out from the group). Skills should be tested often in classes where motivation is lacking.

Methodology for teaching dance is not difficult but does require careful planning. Records are available that talk the class through the moves and then have them dancing. Additional methods include walk-throughs with explanations, sample set demonstrations, and demonstrations of moves by teachers or a demonstration set of teachers. Music should continue as long as there is at least one set still performing. When there are breakdowns, the teacher assists those sets needing additional help. One good way is for the teacher to take someone's place for a few minutes and dance with them, cueing the dancers slightly ahead of the caller. Another is to encourage someone in the group (or the whole group) to cue the set while dancing. If a set is doing really well, that set should have an opportunity to demonstrate for the class. This helps other students to observe a dance performed correctly and gives recognition for a job well done. Completed dances need to be reviewed frequently in order for students to experience daily success. Throughout the entire teaching process, instructions must be thorough and explicit—nothing can be taken for granted.

Evaluations can be in two forms: written and skills. For skills, the teacher can divide a dance into parts for a checklist evaluation. A sample dance might be divided as follows: introduction, 10 points; main figure, 40 points (10 × 4 repetitions); trim, 40 points; and ending, 10 points. Students draw numbers at Laredo Middle School for the order of testing. It is treated like a contest, and the teachers try to make it fun. Groups desiring to go first may do so. While a group is testing, remaining groups may practice their dance, watch, or work on the next dance. Students are appreciative of others' efforts and have been known to applaud after seeing an outstanding effort by their peers.

Written tests may involve such things as parts of a square, position names and places, and parts of a specific dance. Units are ended by evaluating dances that each set invents, writes, practices, calls or memorizes, and performs. The results are usually very rewarding and may make the teacher wonder why square dance has not been taught before.

With modifications, the above methods may be administered with equal success in the teaching of folk and line dance as well.

Rope Skipping

What does one do with a class of seventh and eighth grade girls and boys in a small space in a short period of time with a little bit of money for equipment? One might give rope skipping a try.

A rope skipping unit can be implemented by using one rope for every two or three students (everyone needs a rest once in a while), a clipboard, pencil, paper, and a small room or area to work in. It might be a unit by itself, or it might be a rotational station in another unit in which one needs to limit numbers.

The amount of time used in a rope skipping unit may vary, depending on the number of skills taught and the objectives. Successful units can be as short as three or four days. Objectives may include increasing coordination, timing, endurance, and leg strength, as well as helping students develop an appreciation for rope skipping as an aerobic conditioner for athletics and for personal fitness.

Successful motivation may be achieved by several methods. Simply jumping in place for 20–30 seconds and having the students feel the difference in their own pulse rates facilitates a discussion on aerobic conditioning. Talking about the role of rope skipping in a boxer's life, or as a method of conditioning used by some athletic teams, motivates other students. It may also be pointed out that, in a personal fitness program, skipping rope may be an alternative for the days one cannot ride a bike, run, or swim—that it need not be one's entire program. Included in motivation is the demonstration of the skills presented. It looks like fun, it appears to involve conditioning, and it is definitely challenging. The students' image of rope skipping may be forever changed, and they will be willing to give it a try.

If additional motivation is needed, a skills test may be used. One sample evaluation includes six skills worth a maximum of 10 points each. Three of the skills are relatively simple (forward on two feet, backward on two feet, and forward or back on one foot), and three are a little more difficult (forward crosses, back crosses, and double revolutions). The simple skills require ten consecutive jumps for 10 points. If a student does not complete ten consecutively, the number completed can be recorded. A student may test as many times as desired, the best score always being recorded. The more difficult skills require at least 20 jumps for 10 points (crosses alternate with uncrossed jumps and doubles alternate with singles). A student may take as many jumps between crosses or doubles as wanted but is made aware of the fact that this requires more endurance. Point values for this sample might be 30 points for D, 35 for C, 40 for B, and 45 for A.

As most students have not had much experience in rope skipping skills, the teacher has a rare opportunity to begin with a group having similar abilities. Girls and boys do equally well for this reason. Almost anyone can do the simpler skills with practice, and those who cannot readily do them learn quickly with some help, encouragement, and tips. The more difficult skills require some endurance, patience, and work. An A or B grade is attainable through practice and effort. Students may also increase their success by asking for help, sticking with the task, and being responsible to test on each skill when ready.

Some additional benefits add to the enjoyment of the unit for the instructor and students. The students help and support each other frequently in this activity and share in each other's success. Recognition for skill mastery is given to some students who may not normally excel in traditional activities. All students have the opportunity to experience the satisfaction of achievement through hard work and patience. Many students comment favorably about the unit and the fun they have had. Students who have completed their skills successfully have contributed to the class by helping other students, setting up double-dutch rope games, and showing the class new skills and challenges. If a school is considering a small curriculum change, rope skipping may be the answer.

Affecting Positive Behavior in Nondress Students

Submitted by: Robert Andrew Garcia,
Director, Graduate Programs in Physical Education

School: Stanford University
School of Education
Stanford, CA 94305

Summary

Today in secondary school physical education classes, dress requirements are rarely strict. Educators simply ask students to dress in a comfortable and safe fashion that is conducive to active participation and in a manner appropriate for the specific class activity. Yet, some students refuse to dress for class. Lack of funds to purchase clothing, lack of interest in the activity, and fear of failure are among the reasons for electing to sit and watch.

Because of failure to comply with minimum dress requirements, the nondresser in physical education class poses a problem for educators and school administrators. The nondresser does not contribute to the class environment and many times distracts the teacher as well as the members of the class.

Dealing with and handling nondressers has been a continuous problem for student teachers enrolled in the Stanford Teacher Education Program (STEP). The familiar suggestions were given to encourage all students to participate: (1) proper attire worn by teachers, (2) creative and exciting curriculum content, (3) good instruction and presentation of materials, and (4) open communication between the teacher and students. In addition, the STEP students have tried a technique that has affected nondressers by making them accountable for their time and ultimately has encouraged nondressers to participate in the physical education class.

Outline

The technique requires the nondresser to prepare and present an in-class verbal book report on a topic selected by the teacher. It includes:

I. Identification of students who do not dress for physical education class, particularly students who miss class on a regular basis.

II. Teacher preparation
   A. The teacher must have an assortment of textbooks, journals,

magazines, and other appropriate reading materials concerning the activity.
    B. In advance of class, the teacher must prepare specific topics for the nondresser to research and study.
III. Explanation of task
    A. Teacher gives instructions, so that the nondresser clearly understands what is expected. During the class period, the teacher expects the nondresser to work on a 3–4 minute verbal report on what was learned from the readings and to present this to the class at the end of the period.
IV. Nondresser presentations
    A. At the close of the period, the teacher gathers the class and sets aside 8–10 minutes for the nondressers to report.
       1. Teacher demands silence from the class.
       2. Teacher requires students to be courteous and attentive.
       3. Teacher clarifies and reinforces points made during the presentations.
V. Communication
    A. Teacher shows students the benefits to be derived from the verbal reports.
       1. Nondressers are able to utilize the time spent in class.
       2. Nondressers are able to expand their knowledge about an activity, sport, or game.
       3. The verbal report encourages nondressers to take an active role in physical education class.
VI. Evaluation
    A. Quality of presentations
    B. Number of students who continue to be nondressers.

Description

During their class periods, it became apparent to the student teachers that many

of the nondressers would sit on the sidelines and not pay attention. Usually they would be disruptive to the class or simply not be interested in the day's events. Thus, for a 45-minute class period, nondressers accomplished very little.

In order to facilitate total and active class participation, the student teachers established a course requirement that nondressers prepare an in-class verbal report on a topic selected by the teacher. A report is made at the close of each class period by every nondresser.

This technique has four main objectives: (1) it encourages nondressers to be active participants in the class, (2) it discourages idle use of time by nondressers, (3) it gives the nondresser the opportunity to read and learn about a particular aspect of the activity being taught, and (4) it gives all students the chance to obtain additional knowledge about the activity.

At the close of every class period, a routine is established where the teachers set aside 8–10 minutes to review the day's activities, make appropriate announcements, and listen to the reports of the nondressers.

Conditions Specific to Idea

It is necessary for the teacher to be prepared and to have the appropriate resources for the nondresser to utilize. In addition, the teacher must be conscious of the passage of time so that all nondressers who need to make a report are able to fulfill their assignment. Finally, the teacher must encourage the cooperation of the class so that the other students listen to the presentations.

Evaluation

Upon first learning of the teaching method, the STEP students were apprehensive but quickly found that the results were favorable. Soon after implementation of the verbal report requirement, the nondresser rate declined significantly. As many students stated, "I'd rather dress properly than make an oral report."

Self-Grading to Develop Responsibility and Cooperation

Submitted by: Dr. Dianne Boswell O'Brien*

School: Reidland High School
Paducah, KY 42001

Summary

Responsibility and self-motivation are important behaviors that can be learned in physical education. This article describes self-evaluation, a form of grading. It discusses the implementation of student-teacher planning and student evaluation of skill, effort, and knowledge. These ideas for grading not only develop student responsibility but also peer cooperation. When students are given freedom to set their own objectives and to plan and to implement activities, students feel a responsibility to self and others to see that plans are successfully implemented.

Outline

I. Student-teacher planning
  A. Group discussion in planning the curriculum

B. Individual planning for personal improvement
  C. Group discussion in planning the measurement and evaluation processes
II. Measurement and evaluation
  A. Skill
  B. Effort
  C. Knowledge
III. Grades

Description

The following techniques are successful in helping high school students to become responsible, self-motivating individuals.

Student-Teacher Planning

Developing student responsibility through student-teacher planning involves group discussion and individual planning. Student-teacher planning is an effective way to get students to assume personal responsibility for their actions. Student-teacher planning may also help to improve student achievement.

1. Group discussion in planning the curriculum

*Currently in the Department of Recreation and Physical Education, Murray State University, Murray, Kentucky 42071.

To begin the discussion, the teacher:

    1. Asks the students to put in writing what they expect to gain from taking the class

    2. Asks the students what activities they would enjoy as class experiences

    3. Discusses the positive and negative aspects of various activities such as team games, lifetime sports, fitness training, and rhythms

    4. Discusses the activity possibilities which are available at the school and allows the students to make additions to those activities.

Following this approach to student-teacher planning has fringe benefits. The author found that the students planned and implemented the following activities: badminton when the school had no badminton racquets, swimming when the school had no pool, bowling when the school had no bowling lanes, TV performance by students who had no previous television experience, and a stress challenge course (par course) when they had no outdoor activity area.

2. Individual planning for personal improvement

People, especially teenagers, are interested in themselves. Teenagers are capable of designing plans for their self-improvement and enjoy doing so. When pre-test measurements are made of students at the first of the semester, students can use those pre-test measures to make personal improvement plans for themselves. For example, the teacher measures skinfolds, weight, height, strength, flexibility, and endurance at the first of the semester. Students see the results of their measurements and are asked to evaluate their current status and then design a plan for themselves. During this process, the teacher serves as a resource person, furnishing statistics, measuring devices and alternative activity plans for personal improvement. The key to initiating student responsibility is to have the student make the decisions and be responsible for showing progress.

A typical format for this activity would include the following:

    1. Students take the pre-test.

    2. Teacher and students discuss the results of the pre-test. The teacher asks, "What was your score on the 12-minute run? What could you do to improve your score? Was your score as good as you would like for it to be? Please set a realistic goal for yourself if you would like to improve."

    3. Students set goals for themselves and design an improvement plan. The teacher says, "List the activities which you could use to improve your score. List the duration, intensity, and frequency of those activities. Make a specific list of the activities you will do in class when given 30 minutes free time. Keep in mind your improvement goal."

    4. Students design and implement a plan for reporting progress toward improvement. The teacher performs a systematic weekly check to see if the students are following their plan of action. (Checking indicates that the teacher is interested in the student's progress.) The author uses formal aerobic point sheets which are turned in weekly. High school students who participated in the process improved 14 percentile points in one year in their overall fitness scores on the AAHPERD Youth Fitness Test. (O'Brien, 1979)

3. Group discussion in planning the measurement and evaluation processes

If students are allowed to plan the activities and to set their personal objectives for the class, the logical extension of that process is to let the students plan the measurement and evaluation process. In this planning the teacher first lists on the blackboard *all* the terms that the students feel should be included in the evaluation. Next, the items are listed by categories. In the final step, items are then placed into categories and the categories are given priorities. The usual outcome of this process is that the students want to be evaluated on skill, effort, and knowledge.

Measurement and Evaluation

1. Skill

Students can develop increased self-responsibility through evaluating others as well as themselves. One technique in measuring skill utilizes checklists and charts.

1. The teacher selects one student leader for each activity.
2. The teacher works with the student leader and the other students so that the class is aware of the requirements of skilled performance for a certain activity.
3. The teacher gives checklists containing the student names and activities to the student leader who is in charge of a specific activity.
4. A student who is ready to perform that activity goes to the student leader and tries to perform that activity at the check-off level. Once the student becomes proficient at the skill, the student is given a check. Optional activities are given so that a student does not need to become proficient at all activities.

Standardized skill tests which measure individual sports skills provide another measurement which can be charted for the student. On these tests it may be important for a score to be scaled for the entire class so that the students can compare their test results with those of other classmates. For fitness activities such as the AAHPERD Youth Fitness Test, raw scores and percentile scores are recorded on the charts. Since the test has national norms, the students can compare their scores with those of students of the same age throughout the country. As previously noted, students plan improvement activities and then the test is repeated. The test scores and self-improvement scores are noted on the chart. Student achievement in improved scores, not competition, is the focus.

Many of the activities in physical education are team sports. For these activities, group scores are recorded on the charts. This group score might be a team win in volleyball or a group performance in gymnastics. For example, if the group score was a score of four, each individual received a four. For these events, it is important to strive for balanced teams so that all teams may have equal opportunities for winning and for receiving points for that win.

2. Effort

Discussion and measurement techniques allow students to focus on the cooperative aspects of physical education activities. Students discuss the leadership-followship roles of students immediately after they participate in an activity. For improving cooperation, a discussion of the following questions is helpful:

1. What were the methods specific individuals used to help the team?
2. Why was cooperation important to the team?
3. How was awareness of the feelings of others important?
4. How did you help your team?

Verbalization of the concept of cooperation is important if affective learning (a change of character) is to take place. Immediate feedback discussions and long-term reflections are both important techniques for producing cooperation among students. Following several days of activities, the students complete the following questionnaire, which allows the student to reflect on past experiences and make value judgments. Such value judgments promote affective learning. The questionnaire is kept as a confidential record by the teacher and is later returned to the student at evaluation time. The information is always kept confidential by the student and the teacher.

Confidential Questionnaire

1. I learned _____ from working with my team.
2. This might be helpful to me later in life because _____ ?
3. I was helpful to my team because _____?
4. I was not helpful to my team because _____ ?
5. _____ (name of another student) was most helpful to our team because _____ ?
6. _____ was least helpful to our team because _____ ?
7. I could help (name of another student) by _____ ?

Use of these simple techniques has been very effective in helping students grow as responsible, caring, sharing members of a group. Research with the author's high school students found that, at the end of the year, students in physical education classes had improved their perception of their ability to get along well with others. The control group of similar physical education students actually declined in their perception of their ability to get along well with others. These measurements were taken by pre-tests and post-tests of "How I See Myself," a test of self-concept.

Participation record keeping is part of the self-grading process. During the student planning sessions, students often decide that it is important to participate and that part of their grade should come from participation. To facilitate record keeping, squads are formed. Each squad has a small number of students and a squad leader. The squad leader is responsible for checking roll and seeing that all students in the squad are dressed properly. The squad leader then records the team absentees and dress results on the teacher records. When a grading period arises, the students then use the teacher records to check their own absences and participation times. Dressing or participation is considered "effort" and is part of their grade. Since the students have access to a visual record of their participation, they are then able to evaluate their effort in that area.

3. Knowledge

Health knowledge, sports knowledge, and the application thereof constitute the knowledge portion of self-evaluation. High school students are very capable of designing their own assignments of reading, reporting, and organizing audiovisual aids. In order to review cognitive materials, the students form team groups. In the group, the team leader is responsible for seeing that everyone is active in the discussion. Individual members of the group are responsible for small segments of information. For example, the students may report information they have researched, or they may use movies or filmstrips. The teacher serves as a resource person, making selections for class assignments and helping to organize and find material. The students also design their own test questions and usually consider this a fun activity. To facilitate uniform test construction, the students are given 3 × 5 index cards. They write the test questions on one side of the card and the answers on the other side. Part of the fun comes when the students are allowed to trade cards within their group and to review themselves for the tests. However, actual test construction is the responsibility of the teacher, and a uniform test is taken by the entire class. On some occasions the students may trade papers and grade their own test. Records of these test scores are kept by the teacher. At the end of the evaluation period, students are given the records of their knowledge test scores.

When knowledge groups were used by the author, the side effects were numerous and positive. There were isolates in class who never tried to learn cognitive materials until they were in peer groups. The group learning experiences seemed to work for the students who were just interested in occupying space until they were 16 years of age and could drop out of school. Furthermore, peer pressure was an aid in motivating the students to be more productive.

Grades

At the end of the nine-week grading period, the students are asked to assign themselves grades of A, B, C, D, or F. In addition to self-assigned grades, students are asked to submit a written critique which explains why they deserve that particular grade.

Students prepare a written appraisal of their skill, knowledge, participation, and fitness level. Unless the grade is indefensible, each student receives the self-assigned grade.

In comparing student's grades with teacher-formulated grades for a one-year period, there were only five out of 90 grades that were different. Three of the student self-grades were higher than the teacher's grades and two of the student's grades were lower.

Conditions Specific to Program

It is easy to implement all or part of the ideas for self-grading. However, it is important to establish a democratic classroom environment. In this environment, the students assume some of the work that the teacher often does.

Evaluation

Self-grading has some disadvantages as well as some advantages. Disadvantages are: (1) administrators need to be kept more closely informed of the class activities, and (2) a few students may lack the honesty needed to continue the process.

Self-grading advantages include increased personal responsibility on the part of the student, increased awareness of results on the part of the student, and improved work quality.

PART III
GAMES AND ACTIVITIES IDEAS
Adaptations and Contemporary

Pickle-Ball:
A Net Court Game

Submitted by: Doug Smith, Manager
Pickle-Ball,® Inc.*
3131 Western Ave.
Seattle, WA 98121

Summary

The following letter from a physical educator who includes pickle-ball in the program is typical of the 4,000 letters received:

> As a physical education consultant for several school districts, I am happy to report that pickle-ball has caught on like wildfire at our junior high and high schools. Pickle-ball is also being played at our junior college and state university as part of the intramural program. Our physical educators are teaching pickle-ball units as part of their curriculum and the teachers report that pickle-ball is surpassing volleyball and badminton in popularity. If teachers are seeking a new, inexpensive activity in which the equipment costs are minimal . . . and involves the student in a participation sport that is easy to learn and yields instant self-satisfaction and excitement regardless of athletic ability or strength, then pickle-ball is the game to begin at your school. Our students are playing pickle-ball with relish!

Many teachers have emphasized how effective the game has been in developing the students' reflexes and coordination skills as well as quickness and agility. Students who have hesitated playing racquet games have become enthusiastic about the physical education class when playing pickle-ball, which is a great equalizer for differences in age, sex, strength, and athletic ability.

Pickle-ball is a net court game that is played by two or four people. The court dimensions are identical to a doubles badminton court. The doubles badminton court on the gymnasium floor or outside can be converted to a pickle-ball court simply by lowering the net to three feet. Lightweight paddles and the plastic perforated ball are the keys to producing exciting, long rallies, which consist of volleys at the net and ground strokes similar to tennis. The game involves strategies that include lobbing, overhead slamming, passing drive shots from the baseline, and fast volley exchanges at the net. Pickle-ball is easy to teach and easy to learn and is a coeducational game for all levels.

Outline

Pickle-ball was created in 1965 on Bainbridge Island, near Seattle, Washington. The original purpose of the game was to pro-

---

*Pickle-Ball® is a registered trademark held by Pickle-Ball, Inc., Seattle, Washington.

vide a sport for the entire family, according to the co-inventors: U.S. Congressman Joel Pritchard, William Bell, and Barney McCallum. Initially, families played pickle-ball in their backyards on a hard surface, on driveways, and on street cul-de-sacs. Since the mid-1970s pickle-ball has expanded from a family activity game to a net court game with formalized rules and is currently being played in over 6,000 educational institutions, parks and recreation centers, health clubs, corporate fitness centers, hospitals, and family residences. There are pickle-ball enthusiasts in all 50 states, and many communities and families have annual pickle-ball tournaments.

Description

Pickle-ball rules are similar to those of badminton. At the beginning of a game, both sides rally for serve until a fault occurs, determining which team has the option of serving or receiving first. A doubles team can score a point only when serving. The service must be delivered with an underhand motion, contacting the ball below the person's waist. The server must hit the ball out of the hand and must serve diagonally (cross-court) to the receiver. For the serve to be good, it must clear the 7-foot nonvolley zone and land in the proper service court. If the ball touches the net and still lands beyond the 7-foot nonvolley zone in the proper service court, a let is called and the serve is played over. The ball must bounce once on each side of the net before it can be volleyed in the air during a rally (double-bounce rule). If the ball is going to land in the nonvolley zone, the player can move into the zone before the ball bounces but must let it bounce before returning it.

At the beginning of a game, the team serving first is allowed only one fault before turning the ball over to the opposition. For the rest of the game, both teams serve, alternating court sides, until two faults have been won by the receiving team. After the receiving team wins the serve, the player positioned on the right side of the court always starts serving first. As mentioned before, a team can score points only while serving. A player continues to serve until a fault occurs. In educational settings, matches are the best of three games, with each game played to 11 points. To win, a team must win by 2 points. In singles play, the same basic rules apply, except that one fault results in the loss of service. The court dimensions are the same for singles and doubles.

Pickle-ball being played in the school gymnasium in Seattle, Washington. (Photo by Steven Wilcox)

There are basically four ways to lose a point: (1) hitting the ball out of bounds, (2) hitting the net, (3) stepping into the nonvolley zone and volleying the opposition's return, and (4) volleying the ball in a rally before it has bounced once on each side of the net.

In doubles, the serving team plays back at the baseline because of the double-bounce rule. Again, the serving team cannot charge the net because their opponent's return must bounce first on their side of the court. The receiving team can play one player up at the edge of the 7-foot nonvolley zone and one player back at the baseline. The receiver on the baseline, after hitting a deep return, can advance to the edge of the 7-foot nonvolley zone to join the teammate.

Conditions Specific to Idea

The court dimensions are 20 by 44 feet. This small court area is ideal for converting the doubles badminton court on the gymnasium floor to a pickle-ball court. Utilizing the badminton or volleyball standards, the net is lowered to a height of 36 inches at the standards and hangs 34 inches high in the middle. One advantage of the small court size (one-fifth the area of a tennis court) is that any relatively small space, indoors or out, can be converted to a pickle-ball court. Schools and other institutions have converted gymnasium floors, parking lots, school playgrounds, and tennis courts to pickle-ball courts. Courts can be created with a single can of paint because pickle-ball is easily adaptable to play on any hard surface. Pickle-ball is played on asphalt, concrete, artificial surfaces, and wood floors.

The pickle-ball paddles are made of durable hardwoods and weigh 10–11 ounces. They are made from the strongest lightweight hardwoods available in order to withstand the punishment inflicted on athletic equipment in the school and institutional setting. The head of the paddle is squared off rather than oval. In addition, the head of the paddle may not be strung and no perforations or texturing materials are allowed on the surface. In other words, surfaces with holes, sandpaper, rubber, or glued granules are prohibited.

The ball is a plastic perforated sphere of 3 inches in diameter. The ball will bounce well off any hard surface. The holes in the ball help in slowing down the flight of power shots, much the same way the shuttlecock's feathers slow down the flight of the birdie. It is difficult for one team to dominate as the pickle-ball's flight creates built-in equalizers for the abilities of the opposing players. The rallies are long and exciting, and it is not easy to win a point.

Evaluation

Over 4,000 schools have integrated a 6–8 week pickle-ball unit into the physical education program. Pickle-ball is increasing in popularity because it is easy to learn and teach and, therefore, is quickly enjoyed by students and faculty. Rarely does a participation sport yield instant self-satisfaction the first time it is played, but a novice at pickle-ball will probably reach a fair level of proficiency sooner in this game than in any other sport. Many physical educators are utilizing pickle-ball strategies, tactics, and strokes as preliminary to teaching tennis and badminton skills. Pickle-ball is a game where shot placement, steadiness, patience, and tactics have a far greater importance than power or strength. It also develops eye-hand coordination, flexibility, and quickness. It is a fun game that promotes teamwork, vigorous physical exercise, and pure enjoyment.

General Comments

Four paddles, a net, and a dozen balls are needed for each court. Equipment can be purchased direct from Pickle-Ball, Inc. The strong and durable Diller or Master paddle is recommended for school programs. For more information, write to: Pickle-Ball, Inc., 3131 Western Avenue, Seattle, Washington 98121.

Scurry
Hockey

Submitted by: U.S. Games, Inc.
Box 874 EG
1511 N. Harbor City Blvd.
Melbourne, FL 32935

Summary

This is the hockey players' favorite off-season game, to be played indoors by both boys and girls, men and women.

Outline

This off-season hockey game is brought up to date with safe, modern materials. Any group can play with an absolute minimum of protective equipment. Scurry hockey rules are adapted from ice hockey rules.

Description

Players (either 5 or 6 per team) consist of a center, 1 or 2 wings, 2 defensemen, and a goalie. If there are more than 12 participants, the total number is split into 3 or 4 teams and a team rotates each time a goal is scored. Ideal space required is 100 by 50 feet on a smooth surface. The length should be twice the width. A line or other marker should be used to show the center line. When two teams are playing, three 10-minute periods are best.

Conditions Specific to Idea

The complete scurry hockey game includes 12 scurry sticks of flexible polyvinyl chloride, with protective caps on one end and contoured hand grips with wrist loops on the other, and one ring (a nonstinging circle of foam specially treated to fly over a gymnasium floor). Goals are not included.

Evaluation

Scurry hockey is simple to learn, and it provides a fine opportunity to develop teamwork and skill in stick handling. The ring can be passed and shot with amazing speed, yet it cannot cause injury. The game is simple, safe, and fun.

Scurry hockey being played in the school gymnasium.

Toppleball

Submitted by: U.S. Games, Inc.
Box 874 EG
1511 N. Harbor City Blvd.
Melbourne, FL 32935

Summary

Toppleball can be played indoors or outdoors. It is the only game that permits 15–25 players to participate at one time with equal speed and involvement. It combines teamwork (fielding) with individual play (batting). Because of its simplicity, toppleball can be learned by any group with a minimum of explanation. It is safe and can be played on gymnasium floors, asphalt, concrete, or grass. Since an area only 60 feet by 60 feet is required, space that is generally unusable is adequate.

Outline

Players are placed outside a circle. The first batter is selected and then batters rotate in clockwise direction until everyone bats once. The batter with the most runs at the end of one round wins the game. The batter's objective is to get the maximum number of runs before the toppleball (small ball on batter's post) is dislodged by the playground ball. The batter earns one run by batting the playground ball past the fielder, allowing him to run to the edge of the playing circle and back. The fielder's objective is to get the batter out by knocking the toppleball off the batter's post with the playground ball. Teamwork is the key.

Toppleball being played outdoors on a grassy area. As many as 25 players may play at one time, either indoors or outdoors.

Description

Minimum supervision is required. From 15 to 25 players at age levels of 8 years and up may play. Space required is 60 by 60 feet. Average activity time is 35–60 minutes.

Conditions Specific to Idea

The complete toppleball game includes a toppleball bat, an 8½-inch playground ball, and an indoor/outdoor batter's post constructed of a polyvinyl chloride (PVC) pole with a toppleball at top of a spring-mounted urethane base plate.

Evaluation

Toppleball is played in over 7,500 recreation departments and school systems in all 50 states. Its acceptance continues to grow, since it is a game that permits 15–25 active youngsters to play at one time.

Pillo Polo

Submitted by: U.S. Games, Inc.
Box 874 EG
1511 N. Harbor City Blvd.
Melbourne, FL 32935

Summary

Pillo polo is a safe team sport designed for active play for boys, girls, or coeducational groups from 7 years of age through college.

Outline

Pillo polo is played according to hockey rules, except that in pillo polo there are no red or blue lines and the goalie is allowed to pick up the ball and throw it down the field. This makes goaltending a more important and satisfying position. One referee is all the supervision required.

Description

Players required are 12 plus substitutes. Age levels range from 7 years up. Space required is 50 by 100 feet. Average activity time is 30 minutes to 1 hour. Hockey rules are used for playing pillo polo.

Conditions Specific to Idea

The complete pillo polo game includes 6 yellow and 6 blue pillo polo sticks (31 inches long), two 7-inch foam balls, and a set of official rules. Goals are purchased separately.

Evaluation

No protective equipment is needed as the equipment for pillo polo is made of soft durable foam. The pillo polo stick is now streamlined, enabling easier handling and more delicate ball control, especially for the younger player. Pillo polo has been used as a successful league and intramural activity in many schools and recreation departments throughout the United States. It is a high-activity, high-energy game that constantly generates excitement. Its format increases confidence in children because the danger of being injured is eliminated.

Boys playing pillo polo in gymnasium. Goalie may pick up ball and throw it.

Girls playing pillo polo outdoors.

Scarf Juggling

Submitted by: Dave Finnigan, Director
The Juggling Institute
23004 107th Pl. W.
Edmonds, WA 98020

Summary

Juggling is becoming popular for teaching motor skills, ball handling, and movement in the physical education setting. Because all object-manipulation skills begin simply and proceed gradually toward increased complexity, the seemingly complex skill of juggling can serve as an example for other motor learning activities. Scarf juggling is a method for slowing down the juggling pattern to permit learning at a slower speed and to provide a larger object for grasping. It is effective with regular and special groups at every level from lower elementary grades through college. The objective is for every student to learn the basic juggling pattern and a number of variations by using three nylon scarves.

Outline

Steps in the process of learning to juggle with scarves include:

1. Throwing one scarf from hand to hand with a figure 8 or infinity sign pattern
2. Throwing two scarves so that they cross in front of the student, still following the infinity-sign path
3. Throwing the third scarf when the second reaches the peak, and catching all three scarves
4. Continuous juggling with three scarves
5. Performing alternate moves and tricks
6. Interactive juggling and partner juggling.

Description

Each student starts with a single scarf which is thrown from hand to hand, palm down, using a downward, clawing catch. There are peaks over the left and right shoulders. The right hand throws hit the left-side peak, and vice versa, creating an X across the chest. If the pattern is followed all the way around, a figure 8 or infinity sign can be seen. Helpful words in instruction are: "Throw across as if waving goodby, and catch straight down. Claw like a lion."

As soon as students can throw and catch a single scarf, they should be given a second one. Instructions are: "Throw the first scarf across your chest as in the previous step. When the scarf gets to the top, look at it, and throw the second scarf across in the opposite direction to the same height, but on the opposite side. Catch the first scarf straight down, then catch the second scarf straight down. Remember to throw . . . throw . . . catch . . . catch . . .."

As soon as students can throw and catch two scarves with accuracy, they should be given a third scarf. The first scarf is held in the dominant hand on the fingertips; the second scarf is held in the subordinate hand on the fingertips; and the third scarf is held deep in the dominant hand. Instructions are: "Throw the first scarf; when it peaks, look at it and throw the second scarf. When the second scarf peaks, look at it and throw scarf number three. Number three is just like number one; it crosses the chest and is caught downward, ending up in the opposite hand on the fingertips."

Now the student can continue to juggle. Juggling is like walking. It is a symmetrical movement. Instructions are: "left . . . right . . . left . . . right . . .. Start with the hand that has two objects. Alternate hands. Look at the peaks. Every time a scarf reaches the top, throw the next one from the receiving hand. Every time you throw, name the hand. By counting cadence, give yourself a verbal cue to keep throwing."

Conditions Specific to Idea

The best scarves for this activity are gossamer nylon scarves, about 18 inches square.

They are available from the Juggling Institute or from magic stores and physical education supply houses such as Passon's, Flaghouse, or Juggle Bug, Inc. The unit of instruction can take as little as half an hour with upper grades and college students or as much as 50 minutes with lower elementary students. The unit is recommended for third grade and above. Supplemental instructions and a catalog are available from the Juggling Institute.

Evaluation

The most telling evaluation of the effectiveness of this unit of instruction is the percentage of students who can actually juggle continuously after one session. A secondary evaluation is the number of students who continue to juggle and desire to practice during physical education period.

General Comments

Juggling teaches self-confidence and body awareness as well as giving students a pattern for learning other complex physical skills. Scarf juggling is a safe method for learning, since it has very few failures and slows patterns down measurably. It can lead to other juggling skills or can be an end in itself. It is an effective station in a games unit or can be a week-long unit in itself.

Beanbag Juggling

Submitted by: Dave Finnigan, Director
The Juggling Institute
23004 107th Pl. W.
Edmonds, WA 98020

Summary

This unit is appropriate for students who have accomplished the scarf juggling activity, or for students in grade six and above as an independent activity. Below grade six, the motor skills are usually not adequate to accomplish the objective of continuously juggling with three objects. Successful accomplishment with three scarves can serve as a selection mechanism for those students ready to continue learning juggling skills. The pattern that objects follow in juggling is the same regardless of the object. With beanbags, the speed of descent is far greater than it is with scarves and the student must develop faster reflexes and a more accurate throw. The descending target is smaller, and precision in catching is required. The objective is for every student to be able to juggle continuously for a dozen or more throws, as well as to understand and be able to execute three separate juggling patterns.

Outline

Steps in the process of learning to juggle include:
1. Throwing one beanbag from hand to hand with palm up, in an infinity-sign pattern
2. Learning to begin and end a juggling run by catching on, and throwing from, the fingertips
3. With three bags, to learn to throw and catch two, with appropriate timing, letting the third rest on the heel of the hand
4. When the second beanbag reaches the peak, throwing the third, and catching all three beanbags
5. Continuous juggling with three beanbags
6. Performing alternative moves and tricks
7. Interactive juggling and partner juggling, as well as juggling games.

Description

Each student starts with one beanbag which is thrown from hand to hand, palm upward, using a scooping, underhand throw and a smooth, cushioning catch. There are peaks over the left and right shoulders. The completed pattern might look like a bow tie or like butterfly wings. Helpful words for the instructor to say might be: "Imagine a ray of light coming out of your heart. Scoop under that ray of light, and catch with your other hand, then scoop back under and catch with the original hand. Make an X across your chest. Remember to catch . . . scoop . . . throw . . . catch . . . scoop . . . throw."

As soon as students can throw and catch a single beanbag for ten trials without a drop, they should move on to three beanbags. Two are held on the heels of the hands with the little finger and ring finger. The third is thrown from hand to hand, using a nest formed by the thumb, the index finger, and the middle finger to throw and to catch. This is a warm-up exercise designed to help begin and end the juggling pattern.

Now it is time to exchange two beanbags. The hand that has two beanbags starts. The fingertip beanbag is number one. It is thrown with a scooping underhand toss, as practiced previously. When it reaches the peak, the second beanbag is thrown from the opposite hand with a similar throw. The beanbags cross the chest, peak in succession, and are caught in the order that they are thrown. They end up in opposite hands.

In order to keep juggling, the student needs only to keep throwing to the same height each time, alternate hands, look at the peaks, and count cadence: "right . . . left . . . right . . . left. Keep everything in a plane in front of your body and about one foot away. Don't throw forward out of this plane." This move is called cascade juggling.

Additional beanbag juggling tricks that can be learned in a short time include the reverse cascade (where the beanbags descend into the center, rather than rising from it) and columns (where two beanbags are thrown simultaneously, one from each hand). All juggling tricks proceed from one of these three moves: an underhand throw (the cascade), an overhand throw (the reverse cascade), and columns (where you throw straight up, and each beanbag has its own pathway).

Interactive, or partner, juggling can begin almost immediately. Patterns include take-aways, where two jugglers share a set of beanbags either front to front or side by side, and passing, where two partners share two sets of equipment and throw objects back and forth.

Conditions Specific to Idea

The best beanbags to use for this activity are Juggle Bug cubical beanbags, 2½ inches square. These are available from the Juggling Institute, Passon's, Flaghouse, or local magic stores. This unit of instruction should take about one class period. The best supplemental instruction is *The Joy of Juggling* from Juggle Bug, Inc.

Evaluation

The game may be judged on the basis of how many students learn to juggle and how many want to continue juggling.

General Comments

Beanbag juggling is the second step in a curriculum that can include rings and clubs, interactive juggling, juggling games, and relay races. It can serve as the introduction to a circus arts unit that can include balance, clowning, tumbling, acrobatics, unicycling, and other circus skills. Most important is the sense of accomplishment that comes from learning to juggle successfully.

Volley Tennis

Submitted by: Andy Kostick
Dave Gehler

School: Barrington High School
616 West Main Street
Barrington, IL 60010

Summary

Volley tennis was introduced for a number of reasons: (1) an activity was needed to utilize tennis court space in the early spring when many outside areas are unsuitable for play, (2) an outdoor activity was needed that could be played in cool and cold weather, (3) the addition of volley tennis allowed more space for indoor activity, and (4) the carryover skills from volleyball are identical to most of the skills in volley tennis, thereby diminishing the amount of time needed for actual instruction.

Volley tennis fits a coeducational class very well and, in some respects, allows more participation by girls. Units can be scheduled for varying lengths of time (i.e., 2–4 weeks depending upon other scheduling variables inherent to a given program). Volley tennis is a transitional activity which can best be used when weather is too inconsistent to schedule activities outside on a daily basis.

Outline and Description

I. Statement of purpose
   A. Instruction in volley tennis is included to introduce and develop skills, knowledge, and acceptable safety practices for the participation and enjoyment of a recreational game. Volley tennis gives students another activity that can be played on a tennis court.

II. Scope
   A. Fundamentals of the game are taught on all levels through the medium of the game and instructor-designated drills and tests.

III. Objectives
   A. To teach rules of the game.
   B. To teach game strategy.
   C. To review and develop the following game skills:
      1. Serving
      2. Passing
      3. Receiving (bump) and setting
      4. Spiking
      5. Dinks
   D. To teach game safety.

E. To teach students an informal co-educational activity that can be played on a recreational basis.

IV. Related information
   A. Equipment
      1. Volleyball
      2. Tennis court and net
   B. Playing area
      1. Tennis court doubles area
      2. Net height identical to tennis net height.
   C. Teams
      1. Teams consist of 5 or 6 contestants. Six players are ideal, but more can be used.
      2. Player positions (6 per team)
         a. Two net players, playing about 4 feet inside the boundary lines and about 4 feet back of net. Their function is to spike and play short volleys (including dinks).
         b. Two mid-court players, positioned in the doubles alley.
         c. Two back court players, positioned on or near the baseline of the court. Each player covers half of the doubles court. Their function is to play volleys and spikes that elude net and mid-court players.
   D. Serving
      1. Volley for serve for first game. The winner of the volley may serve or elect to begin play with the wind.
      2. All serves should be made from behind the baseline unless excessive wind is a problem. If the wind is too strong, the service area may be moved forward at the instructor's discretion.
      3. The overhand, underhand, or underhand serve with one bounce may be used.

      4. Serve may land in any portion of the opponent's court.
      5. Serve may not bounce over net.
      6. Ball must be served over net on fly.
      7. Server continues to serve as long as his side earns points. Points may be scored by serving team only.
   E. Rules of play
      1. Ball may be played off the volley or off a bounce. Playing the bounce is recommended.
      2. Ball-handling violations include throws, carries, and catches.
      3. Game consists of 15 points. A team must win by 2 or more points.
      4. Whenever a total of 10 points is scored (7–3, 6–4, 5–5, etc.), teams change sides, but the person serving remains the server. Scoring continues in sequence.
      5. Ball that lands on boundary line is considered in play.
      6. Ball may be played off volley or bounce.
      7. Ball may pass over the net after the first, second, or third player contact. A maximum of three hits is allowable.
      8. Ball may bounce before each player contact.
      9. Ball cannot be bounced over net.
     10. If ball hits player unintentionally and rebounds over the net, regular play must continue.
     11. Intentional kicking of ball is a violation.
     12. Player rotation must occur. A Z-type rotation is recommended.
     13. If ball bounces within the court boundary lines and rebounds outside the court, play may continue.

Giant Relay

Submitted by: Charlene E. Thomas
Debbie Cates

School: All Saints' Episcopal School
Confederate Ave.
Vicksburg, MS 39180

Summary

This special event is designed to involve as many students as possible in a continuous relay, including skills students have learned in physical education classes and other activities. The relay is coeducational, with emphasis on teamwork, skill, enjoyment, and participation. It is an exciting experience with 48 activities, in which each team must select the most skillful members to participate for each event. The relay consists of 77 participants for each team, totaling 154 students.

All Saints' Episcopal School's enrollment is 185 students in grades 8–12. The school is divided into two intramural teams, the Angels and Devils, which compete in various activities and sports (the giant relay, spelling bee, academics, poster competition, skits, and 30 different sports). The team winning the giant relay gains 150 points, and the losing team gains 75 points for effort.

Outline

  I. Rules of the relay
 II. List of events (48)
III. Description of events

Description

Rules

1. Each event must be completed in order according to the official copy of the giant relay. No event may be skipped or moved out of order.
2. Each event must be completed correctly before the next event can begin. There is a 15-minute time limit on each event. If the task cannot be performed within the time limit, the team may proceed to the next event at a signal from the supervising staff member.
3. Only students on the official roster may participate in the relay and only in the event for which they are scheduled.
4. Students should be at the location of their event at 3:30 p.m. (the start of

the relay) and remain there until they have completed their event.

5. The 15-minute time limit does not apply if a student is not present to perform in that event.

6. Each participant must have the team flag in possession before beginning the event.

7. Any deviation from rules may lead to total disqualification of the offending team from the relay.

8. The supervising staff members are in charge of the individual events. They see that each competitor for the Angel or Devil teams performs the event in an identical manner and decide when the event has been performed correctly and completely.

Events

Below are listed the events, with location and number of participants from each team in parentheses:

1. Run from starting line to archery field (swing set—1)
2. Pop 5 balloons (archery field—1)
3. Run to soccer goal by woods (archery field—1)
4. Dribble around cones (soccer goal—1)
5. Shoot and make four goals from free shot area and run to starting line on track (soccer goal—1)
6. Run mile relay (starting line on track—4)
7. Run to gymnasium center court (starting line on track—1)
8. Shoot and make five free throws and take flag to mats (basketball court—1)
9. Do four consecutive forward rolls and take flag to mats (center circle of gymnasium—1)
10. Do five consecutive good serves over volleyball net and give flag to circle (volleyball court—1)
11. Do 25 consecutive hits in circle drill and give flag to jump roper (volleyball court—6)
12. Jump rope 25 consecutive times (volleyball court—1)

13. Run to monkey bars (volleyball court—1)
14. Walk monkey bars on hands from one end to the other without letting go (monkey bars—1)
15. Run to canoe trailer (monkey bars—1)
16. Unrack canoe and carry to pool (pool—2)
17. Launch canoe into pool, paddle to center with hands, change positions, paddle to other side and get out (pool—2)
18. Enter canoe, spin canoe three times to the right and three times to the left, paddle to the other side and get out (pool—2)
19. Take canoe out of pool, carry to canoe trailer, and rack (pool—2)
20. Run to tents in Dell area (canoe trailer—1)
21. Put up tent (Dell area—2)
22. Take tent down and return all parts to bag (Dell area—2)
23. Run from Dell to snack bar door (Dell area—1)
24. Lay and light a fire to burn through string (outside pavillion—1)
25. Roast marshmallow and eat it (outside pavillion—1)
26. Run inside pavillion and draw a picture of Father Dickson, Ike, and Sparky (outside pavillion—1)
27. Splint arm, put on a sling, and take flag to pool (pavillion—2)
28. Throw frisbee across pool to partner five times (ten in all) (pool—2)
29. Walk backwards up paved road (pool—1)
30. Ride bike to tennis courts on road (top of hill—1)
31. Do five good serves into each service court (tennis courts—1)
32. With partner, rally ball ten times without missing in singles court (tennis courts—2)
33. Run to softball field (tennis courts—1)
34. Batter hit three balls to person in outfield; outfielder return ball to batter after each hit (softball field—2)

35. Run to archery field (softball field—1)
36. Make a pyramid (archery field—6)
37. Run to center circle of basketball court in gymnasium (archery field—1)
38. Play "around the world" and run to mats (center circle, gymnasium—1)
39. Do four consecutive cartwheels and take flag to badminton court (mats in gymnasium—1)
40. Rally shuttlecock ten consecutive times with partner and take flag to ladder (badminton court—2)
41. Tie a swiss seat on yourself and untie it (gymnasium—1)
42. Tie a bowline around your waist, untie it, and run to TV room (gymnasium—1)
43. Play on the recorder (TV room—1)
44. Run to track (TV room—1)
45. Ride mile bicycle relay (track—4)
46. Run to archery field (track—1)
47. Shoot 25 points from 20 yards with six arrows (archery field—1)
48. Run to finish line by swing set (archery field—1)

Conditions Specific to Idea

Facilities
1. Soccer field
2. Track
3. Archery field
4. Gymnasium
5. Swimming pool
6. Pavillion
7. Tennis court
8. Softball field

Equipment for Each Team
1. Bandana handkerchiefs (flag)
2. Balloons
3. Cones
4. Tent
5. Matches, string, and marshmallow

6. Paper and pencil
7. Splint and triangle bandage
8. Frisbee
9. Bicycle
10. Tennis racquet and ball
11. Softball bat and ball
12. Tumbling mats
13. Badminton racquet and shuttlecocks

To start the relay each team represented must have the "team flag" at the completion of an event and must pass the flag to the next competitor. This continues throughout the relay; therefore, the flag must pass the finish line in order for a team to win.

The entire faculty and staff are involved in supervising each specific event. The relay requires 45–60 minutes.

Evaluation

Strengths
1. Large number of participants
2. Excellent physical activities
3. Varied skills involved
4. Teamwork and team spirit
5. All facilities used
6. Involves physical education, music, and art
7. Self-motivation (each student can excel in favorite area)
8. Both winning and losing teams are awarded points.

Weakness
Pressure to complete each event

General Comments

In order for the giant relay to be a success, organization is the main factor. Each supervisor is responsible for the equipment and materials necessary for the event being supervised. The giant relay could be adapted to fit any program, utilizing the equipment and facilities available.

Gymnastic Septathlon

Submitted by: Dr. Ernest J. Gershon,
Professor Emeritus

School: University of Wisconsin-LaCrosse
LaCrosse, WI 54601

Summary

An occasional play day or stunt day may add a little zest to the unit in gymnastics. Seven stunts are presented here; they have been used successfully with over 2,000 men and 300 women in physical education classes at LaCrosse for several years. This septathlon usually takes place the last day before a vacation or before a break in the schedule. Data collected are transposed into achievement scales on a computer, but hand computations would suffice.

Outline

The seven stunts are:
1. Bar snap for distance.
2. Pullups on the jump high rings.
3. Rope climb (24 feet).
4. Bar vault for height.
5. Backward broad jump.
6. Handstand in circle.
7. Horizontal bar swinging shot put.

Description

The stunts, with instructions to students, are:

1. *Bar snap for distance.* Bar is 60 inches high. Grasp bar, jump to underswing and at forward end of swing release grasp and snap to stand, striving for distance. Score is in inches for the best of three attempts.

2. *Pullups on the jump high rings.* Jump to straight arm hang. Bend arms until ears are visible through the openings in the rings. Lower to straight arm hang. Repeat. Score is the number of complete pullups performed as described.

3. *Rope Climb* (24 feet). From standing position on mat with hands grasping rope, begin climb without using feet against the mat. Climb to touch beam. Score is in seconds and tenths.

4. *Bar vault for height.* Adjust bar to about chest height, or lower, at the start. Grasp bar with both hands, jump, and vault over the bar without touching the bar with any part of the body except the hands. (A front vault is recommended.) Continue to adjust

the bar upward after each successful vault. Score is the highest vault in inches. Three attempts are permitted at each height.

5. *Backward broad jump.* Stand with heels to the mark and jump backward for distance. Measure jump from nearest landing mark to starting line in inches. Score is the best of three trials.

6. *Handstand in circle.* The circle is three feet in diameter. Place hands in circle and kick up to handstand. Score is in seconds from the time the second foot leaves the floor until either foot strikes the floor or at the time the performer departs from the circle. (Performer may move around on hands while in the circle.)

7. *Horizontal bar swinging shot put.* Adjust bar to jump height. Jump to hang. Partner places basketball between the feet and ankles of the performer. Take a long underswing forward, backward, and on next forward swing release the basketball. Score is the distance of the shot put to the nearest foot, recording the best of three attempts.

Conditions Specific to Program

1. Mats are provided. Safety of equipment and set-up must be checked.
2. Spotting is required on all stunts.
3. Score sheets and pencils are provided.
4. Timers, chalk, measuring tapes, and a basketball are provided.

Evaluation

1. Raw scores are collected for each event.
2. The mean and the standard deviation are calculated for each event for boys and for girls.
3. For each event for boys and for girls, an achievement scale (0–100) is constructed in steps of ten (or any number of steps, by adjusting the formula).
   a. The mean is placed opposite the scale score of 50.
   b. The standard deviation is multiplied by six and divided by ten. This provides an increment for

finding the raw score equivalents for all of the other scale scores. For example, to find the raw score for a scale score of 60, the increment is added to the raw score that appears opposite the scale score of 50 (mean). To find the raw score equivalent for a scale score of 70, the increment is added to the raw score that is opposite the scale score of 60. This process continues until all the scale scores through 100 are determined. To find the raw score equivalent for a scale score of 40, the increment is subtracted from the raw score that is opposite the scale score of 50 (mean). The process continues in a like manner until all scale scores through zero have been matched with raw scores. This procedure must be reversed for the rope climb event, in which the lowest score is the best score.

4. When the student obtains a score on any event, this score is circled on the individual score chart.
5. Upon completion of the septathlon, the student may connect the circled scores with straight lines, thus indicating a profile of importance. The scale scores permit evaluation from event to event. Should the student repeat the septathlon at a later time, comparisons in progress may be made.

Strengths
1. The septathlon is fun.
2. Student performs at own rate, selecting any or all stunts.
3. Personal evaluation of performance is available immediately.
4. Student has personal record to take home.
5. A free social spirit is encouraged.
6. Teacher may provide aid and instruction at will.
7. The septathlon can be performed with a large class (30 or more).
8. The idea is adaptable for other units, such as basketball, baseball, or tennis.

Example of Score Chart

Scale Score	Bar Snap for Distance		Pullups		24-ft. Rope Climb		Bar Vault for Height		Backward Broad Jump		Handstand		Horizontal Bar Shot Put	
	F	M	F	M	F	M	F	M	F	M	F	M	F	M
100	75	104	7	21	20	10	59	78	50	78	11	11	44	50
90	69	96		19	24	13	57	75	47	75	10	10	40	46
80	63	88	6	17	28	16	55	72	44	72	9	9	36	42
70	57	80		15	32	19	53	69	41	69	8	8	32	38
60	51	72	5	13	36	22	51	66	38	66	7	7	28	34
50	45	64	4	11	40	25	48	63	35	63	6	6	24	30
40	39	46	3	9	44	28	47	60	32	60	5	5	20	26
30	33	48		7	48	31	45	57	29	57	4	4	16	22
20	27	40	2	5	52	34	43	54	26	54	3	3	12	18
10	21	32		3	56	37	41	51	23	51	2	2	8	14
0	15	24	1	1	60	40	39	48	20	48	1	1	4	10

Weaknesses
1. Some of the stunts may prove to be too difficult for some students.
2. Vigilance is required to prevent dangerous situations from arising.
3. Considerable preparation is necessary, such as provisions of individual record forms, pencils, floor markings, measuring tapes, timers, chalk, and a basketball.

PART IV
ALTERNATIVE
CONTENT
IDEAS
Curricular
Nontraditional
Activities

Teaching Stress Management

Submitted by: Dr. Gretchen Koehler

School: Gustavus Adolphus College
St. Peter, MN 56082

Summary

First aid, general health, cardiopulmonary resuscitation (CPR), and nutrition are no longer the only personal safety and wellness courses being taught in secondary school health and physical education programs. Stress management is an important area worthy of regular class status, and student interest is high in regard to this very personal topic. A suggested course outline for a five-day-a-week, four-week unit is presented here. Topic areas, references, and student assignments are discussed.

Outline

I. *Introduction.* Define stress; give examples of emotional, mental, physical, chemical, environmental, and social stressors; discuss Hans Selye's general adaptation syndrome and the flight-fight response. (2 days)

II. *Relaxation Response.* Instruct and practice deep breathing techniques, progressive muscle relaxation, autogenetics, meditation, visualization, yoga, and stretching exercises. (6 one-half lessons or 3 days—used in connection with lecture for one-half lessons)

III. *Health Habits.* Review important aspects of exercise, diet, and recreation as stress reducers.

IV. *Promoters of Stress.* Discuss the role of Type A personality, sugar, alcohol, drugs, and tobacco as stressors. (2 days)

V. *Stress Diseases.* Review hypertension, cancer, migraine headaches, and arthritis as diseases that can be caused by stress. (3 days)

VI. *Discussion.* Lifestyle changes and coping techniques, such as diet, exercise, meditation, and other relaxation techniques as listed in II. (2 days)

VII. *Other.* Testing, reports, guest lectures, and films. (5 days)

VIII. *References*
Magazine:
   American Health Fitness of Body and

Mind, Box 100034, Des Moines, Iowa 50347

Books

1. *Guide to Stress Reduction,* by L. John Mason, Peace Press, 3828 Willat Ave., Culver City, California 90230
2. *Fit or Fat,* by Covert Bailey, Houghton Mifflin Co.
3. *The Relaxation Response,* by Herbert Benson, Avon Books, New York, New York
4. *Stress Without Distress,* by Hans Selye, New American Library, New York, New York
5. *Mind as Healer, Mind as Slayer,* by Kenneth R. Pelletier, Dell Publishing Co., Inc., New York, New York
6. *Managing Teacher Stress and Burnout,* by Dennis Sparks and Janice Hammond, AAHPERD, 1900 Association Drive, Reston, Virginia 22091
7. *Stress Management for Sport,* by Dr. Leonard D. Zaichkowsky and Dr. Wesley E. Sime, AAHPERD, 1900 Association Drive, Reston, Virginia 22091

Films

"Managing Stress, Anxiety and Frustration"—Human Relations Media, Pleasantville, New York 10570

Topics on loop film:
1. What Is Stress?
2. Stress and the Body
3. Relaxation Techniques
4. Life Management Skills

IX. *Student Assignments*
1. Report in small groups on stress topic of student's choice or as related to class discussion. Students can read magazine articles or appropriate chapters from books and write a brief report to be shared.
2. Write a report on personal stresses and ways of coping.

Conditions Specific to Program

Individual instructors need to structure their lessons per topic. Many references exist besides those listed above. Guest lecturers (experts) can be invited for specific topics and laboratories.

Evaluation

This timely topic is of great interest to students. Personalized assignments and information-sharing discussion groups aid learning and stimulate enthusiasm.

General Comments

There are unlimited possibilities for using the stress management teaching outline for elementary school programs as well as for adult or continuing education programs.

Skeletal Alignment and Injury Prevention for Athletes

Submitted by: Nan Byrd Smith

School: The Holton-Arms School
7303 River Road
Bethesda, MD 20817

Summary

Skeletal Alignment and Injury Prevention for Athletes is the title of an experimental course designed to meet the needs of all sophomores who are selected for an interscholastic sport team, the cheerleading squad, or a performing dance group. Now in its second year, the course meets twice a week for one trimester and fulfills the regular physical education requirement. Its basic purpose is to impress upon athletes the importance of understanding the function of the musculoskeletal system and the ways in which mechanical efficiency and safety in athletics can be increased.

At Holton-Arms, a college preparatory school for girls, sophomores were identified as the student population most likely to benefit from the course. At this age, most students have chosen the interscholastic activity in which they wish to specialize and have attained the intellectual maturity to conceptualize about movement principles and ideokinetic theories. Introduction of the course at this level also provides the coaching and teaching staff with ample opportunities to informally observe and evaluate the impact on the athletic performance of juniors and seniors. It should be noted that course content could easily be modified to be appropriate at another grade level.

Outline

The approximately 20 class sessions are fairly equally divided between lectures or discussion and laboratory experiences. During the laboratory, or activity sessions, students have the opportunity to attempt to apply the principles covered in class discussion. Selection of specific motor skills is based on student interest and area of specialization. For example, Lecture Session 3 involves a discussion of the conversion of momentum from horizontal to vertical and maintaining balance while making a rapid change of direction. The following laboratory session involves four stations requiring these elements of agility: vertical jump and reach, basketball lay-up shot, dodge run, and shuttle run. The discoveries made by the students exploring these activities then become the basis for the next lecture session.

Description

Objectives and Expected Outcomes
1. Each student will be able to demonstrate a working understanding of the joints of the body, their range of motion, their relative stability and mobility, and the connective tissue (muscles, tendons, and ligaments) involved in movement at that joint.
2. Each student will be able to demonstrate examples of specific conditioning techniques that will develop strength and flexibility of antagonistic muscle groups at each body segment.
3. Each student will be able to explain the laws of gravity and motion which influence the mechanics and technical execution of selected skills within their activity.
4. Each student will be more aware of structural limitations, individual muscular strengths and weaknesses, and those body segments or articulations which may be subject to athletic injury.
5. Each student will have an understanding of neuromuscular release, relaxation techniques, and the importance of mental rehearsal in developing motor skills.
6. Each student will be able to explain and demonstrate the principles of static and dynamic alignment and will be aware of how the application of these principles can produce greater mechanical efficiency in performance and minimize the risk of athletic injury.

Course Content and Learning Activities
1. Review of the human skeleton, its major articulations, and primary muscle groups at each segment
2. Analysis of the individual student's body posture, spinal alignment, and postural muscle imbalance, using the Skan-O-Graf, spinal tracings, and diagnostic exercises
3. Discussion of the importance of warm-up and cool-down exercises for prevention of common athletic injuries
4. Review of the principles of motor efficiency in daily life and athletic activities: absorption of shock, positioning to utilize the strongest muscles to do a given task, maintenance of spinal alignment, recovery of balance, control of momentum, correct application of force, etc.
5. Discussion of the most common athletic injuries peculiar to specific sports (e.g., "boot-top" fracture, shin splints, tennis elbow); preventative techniques and exercises
6. Written analysis and demonstration of a specific motor skill, chosen by the student; videotape playback to class for discussion
7. Discussion and practice of conscious neuromuscular relaxation techniques, including progressive relaxation and imagery; relationship to mental rehearsal and application to sports performance and skill

Visual Aids
1. Fully articulated human skeleton
2. Flash cards on bones and muscles (Diane Furman)
3. Anatomical charts (Anatomical Chart Company)
   a. Neuromuscular system
   b. Skeletal system
   c. Vertebral column
4. Videotape
5. Skan-O-Graf

References
1. *Kinesiological Analysis* (unpublished), by N. S. Byrd
2. *The Body* (Life Science Library, Time, Inc., New York)
3. *Sports Doctor's Fitness Book for Women*, by John Marshall, et al., Dell Publications, New York
4. *Stretching for Athletics*, by Dennis Jackson, Leisure Press, New York
5. *Building Sound Bones and Muscles*, by Oliver Allen, Time-Life, New York

6. *The Simon and Schuster Book of Anatomy and Physiology*, by James Bevan, Beazley Publications, New York
7. *Human Movement Potential*, by Lulu Sweigard
8. *The Thinking Body*, by Mabel Todd
9. *Kinesiology: Scientific Basis of Human Motion*, by Katherine Wells

Evaluation

Students are evaluated by the standard Holton-Arms grading criteria: pass/fail, with an effort grade of 1–5 (5 = excellent, 3 = average, etc.). The effort grade is a reflection of the student's performance in analytical and laboratory activities. In addition, each student is required to keep a journal throughout the trimester, logging insights or specific pieces of information that are particularly meaningful to her.

Long-Range Evaluation

The athletes in the classes of 1984, 1985, and 1986 will be given a questionnaire designed to elicit suggestions, strengths, and weaknesses of the course, as well as student perception of its value and impact on athletic performance.

At present, the following positive outcomes are evident:

1. Students approach their coaches more often with specific questions about their performance (e.g., Should I bend my knees more? How can I improve my . . .?).
2. Students verbally acknowledge the importance of adequate warm-up and seem to be more aware of the need for stretching and conditioning before team practices or competition.
3. Students seem more willing to seek help from the staff and from the school nurse concerning suspected injuries and proper treatment.
4. Students seem better able to identify exercises that are potentially dangerous, especially to the lower back and knees. They seem to recognize the importance of avoiding these activities.

Individualized Coeducational Aerobic Dance

Submitted by: Maxine Davis
Teresa Lee Snyder

School: Eastern Washington University
Cheney, WA 99004

Summary

Each student in an aerobic dance unit will progress through skill levels at a different pace, and the program described here allows the student to do this with a sense of freedom and success. Also, because cardiovascular fitness varies so greatly among individuals, it is important to offer a unit which will both challenge the student and permit progression at a safe rate for the individual's physical condition. This unit is designed to provide a relaxed social atmosphere and to allow for little or no failure, as conditioning and simple movement are the primary objectives instead of high skill levels. Below are listed the primary objectives of the program.

Psychomotor Objectives
1. Develop a more efficient cardiovascular system.
2. Develop better relaxation ability.
3. Enhance strength, flexibility, coordination, agility, and balance.
4. Tone muscles.
5. Master locomotive skills.
6. Master locomotive skills in sequence to form aerobic dances.

Cognitive Objectives
1. Understand why and how aerobics improves body functions.
2. Gain satisfaction in learning to move body in rhythmic way.
3. Define and explain aerobic dance.

Outline

   I. Knowledge objectives
     A. Explanation
     B. Activities
     C. Test
  II. Warm-up technique objectives
     A. Explanation
     B. Activities
     C. Test
 III. Cool-down technique objectives
     A. Explanation
     B. Activities
     C. Test

Description

The student begins working with Objective I (as listed in outline) and progresses in sequence, as one objective builds upon the next. To accomplish the objective, the student:

1. Reads and comprehends the objective.
2. Reads directions and/or views videotape of that skill objective.
3. Works on skills under direction of teacher or student aide.
4. Goes to teacher to be tested.
5. Executes 75 percent of the skills in a satisfactory manner. If the objective has not been reached, student receives additional instructions, is given time to correct errors and to practice, and then has chance to retest.

The dances for Objectives IV–XIV would be choreographed and designed by each teacher to suit the specific group. The teacher would choreograph a combination of aerobic and locomotor movements which would repeat approximately three times during an average song. That would be the first aerobic dance. Each dance should fit most moderate tempos whether rock, pop, or country music is used, so that each day only one tape or record player is going. Whether working on Objective IV or X, the student can work to the same music. For variety, music can be changed at times during the class period or each new day. Regardless of which objective the student is working on, after accomplishing Objectives I–III, the student should do the learned warm-up at the start of each class and the cool-down at the end of each class for safety reasons. Correct monitoring of pulse rates should be stressed each day so that students can see their own progress in cardiovascular conditioning.

Below are presented sample warm-up and cool-down routines and a sample aerobic dance:

Warm-up Routine
1. 4 slow head rolls to right; 4 slow head rolls to left; 4 fast head rolls
2. 4 shoulder rolls forward and 4 shoulder rolls back
3. Reach overhead and stretch; release (repeat 4 times).
4. Side stretches: 4 right and 4 left
5. Waist twist: 4 right and 4 left
6. Reach overhead, bend forward (flat back), and hold 8 counts; touch floor with flat palms and hold 8 counts; roll up one vertebra at a time (repeat).
7. Sit on floor, with legs straight in front; reach over and touch toes (flat back) and hold 8 counts; roll up one vertebra at a time; reach over and touch toes (flat back) and hold 8 counts with feet flexed.
8. Straddle legs and stretch forward (flat back) and hold 8 counts; stretch to right side (flat back) and hold 8 counts; stretch to left side (flat back) and hold 8 counts.
9. Hurdle stretch: 8 counts left leg and 8 counts right leg
10. Ankle rolls: 8 counts

Cool-down Routine
1. Take deep breaths in and out continually
2. Walk in large circle moving right in step to music beat
   a. While you walk:
      arm circles 4 forward
      arm circles 4 back
      swing arms in and out for 8 counts
      swing arms up and down for 8 counts
   b. Face front:
      8 heel lifts
      8 toe touches
      8 side touches
      8 reach-ups
3. Repeat this over and over until music ends. Remember: breathe in and out!

Conditions Specific to Program

In developing an aerobic course for a co-educational setting, it is advisable first to consider giving a sample demonstration in traditional men's classes to spur interest. The course itself is not taught any differently when men attend other than exclusion of any highly feminine movements.

Aerobic Dance

Title: "Let's Hang On"
Music by: Barry Manilow
Choreographed by: Teri Snyder

Locomotor Skills: Hop, run, and slide
Difficult Steps: Chasse, pony

Feet	Arms
1. Twist body left	Reach right hand up to left side, left hand on hip
Touch right toe	Touch with left hand
4 twists	Straight down—snap as you twist body
Repeat starting right, then left, right	
2. Lift right knee, hop right	Bend elbows freely
Lift left knee, hop left	
4 heel lifts	Alternate bending elbows, hands to chest
Repeat	
3. 2 skates right	Bent elbows, push both arms to right side
2 skates left	Bent elbows, push both arms to left side
4 travel bends	Straight up, then drop to thighs 4 times
4. 3 jogs forward	Relax arms
1 bounce	Clap overhead twice
3 jogs back	Relax arms
1 bounce	Clap overhead twice
Repeat	
5. Knee lift and kick right	Hands on hips
Knee lift and kick left	Hands on hips
4 bounces on right foot	Arm circles 4 times (horizontal)
4 bounces on left foot	Arm circles 4 times (horizontal)
4 chasses (slides) forward	Swing freely
2 ponies	Swing left arm forward, then right arm
4 bounces backing up	Push arms from in front out to sides

6. Repeat starting at 1–5 until music ends.

Needed equipment includes a videotape of all skills objectives to be performed, a tape recorder, and music. Student aides should be used in class and to film the videotape.

Many resources are available to the beginning instructor. It might be useful to start by taking an aerobic dance class at a recreation center, YMCA, or a private company. Records are available with music especially for aerobics, and many include choreographed dances with instructions (for example, Jackie Sorenson's aerobic dance record). Several books that are available give pictures and instructions for dances and aerobic exercises and physiological background concerning aerobics. These include *Aerobic Dance—A Way To Fitness*, by Mazzeo, *The Aerobic Way*, by Kenneth Cooper, M.D., and *Jane Fonda's Workout Book*, by Jane Fonda.

For the in-service workshop for instructors, several other adult aerobic instructors are needed to assist. Students are not a good choice because faculty may feel threatened by the students' presence. After explaining aerobic principles and teaching them how to monitor pulse rates, the participants are divided into mixed groups and work five minutes each, progressing through three stations that would emphasize upper body, lower body, and abdominal warm-ups. At the end of the 15-minute warm-up, they would begin learning a series of mini-aerobic dances. The next step would be to bring everyone together for a cool-down session. Finally, a short written quiz should be taken to see what material was learned. At the very end, an entire aerobic dance could be demonstrated and the difference between this and aerobic exercises could be pointed out.

Evaluation

Strengths

1. All basic locomotor movements necessary in aerobic dance can be carried over directly to many other sports and activities.
2. Music tends to be a good motivational factor in exercise.
3. Partners of mixed sex can be used, and this is also a motivational technique.
4. Aerobic dance is not highly structured. Dances can easily be adapted to group size, ability, student handicaps, and available music.
5. Aerobic dance is an excellent supplement to all athletic conditioning programs.
6. High skill level is not necessary.

Weaknesses

1. Individual observation of students is a problem.
2. Choreographing dances can be difficult at first.
3. Having one videotape of all skills may stall students' progress while waiting to view demonstrations.
4. Amount of cardiovascular conditioning depends on student motivation.
5. It can be difficult to supervise correct monitoring of pulse rates among students.

General Comments

Aerobic dance is unique because it is a creative, ever-changing, learning process that can be a life-long activity for an individual or a group. Sex, size, handicaps, and skill level are nonhindering factors to success.

The most important key to success for the instructor is motivation, but the nature of aerobic dance is such that participants become motivated without realizing it. Above all, aerobic dance is designed for fun.

Women's Self-Defense and Sexual Assault Prevention

Submitted by: Joan Nelson
Carol Harding

School: Michigan State University
East Lansing, MI 48824

Summary

Today, there is hardly a school, neighborhood, or community that is not concerned about the growing incidence of sexual and domestic violence. Most often, this violence is directed toward women, children, and the elderly. Although the issue of violence is extremely complex and long-term strategies for ending or preventing it are the subject of wide debate, there is little question about the immediate need to equip potential victims with maximum resources and skills for insuring their safety.

Physical educators are in a unique position to offer a combination consciousness-raising and skill-building program of self-defense training. Specific objectives of such a program are:

1. To provide accurate information about the nature and circumstances of violent crimes such as rape and battering
2. To increase participants' skills in analyzing potentially dangerous and assaultive situations in order that they may choose, wisely and quickly, the safest course of action
3. To offer realistic suggestions and guidance for reducing one's vulnerability and accessibility to assailants
4. To provide an opportunity to learn and to perfect a range of self-defense tactics, including physical, verbal, and psychological techniques
5. To make available information on relevant medical and legal procedures involving victims of sexual and domestic violence
6. To encourage the organization of neighborhood or school groups to develop community (as opposed to individual) action strategies for ending violence

Outline

I. Theoretical Instruction
It is important early on to provide (a) an analysis of the causes of crimes of violence against women and children, and (b) accurate information

about the nature and circumstances of these crimes in order to offset widespread myths and misconceptions.

II. Strategies

This involves an examination of common stages of assault and the strategies that might be appropriate. It is most helpful to introduce recent criminal justice data that demonstrates which strategies are more likely to result in successful deterrence of assailants and why. Specific situational factors need also be be examined for how they influence responses to assault.

III. Tactical Instruction

Instruction in actual techniques begins with identification of vulnerable targets and body weapons. Basic strikes, blocks, kicks and evasive footwork are introduced. Basic self-defense instruction should also include confrontation training (verbal and psychological techniques) as well as some discussion about "special assaultive situations," i.e., armed assaults, assaults involving more than one attacker.

Description

The suggested format for a ten-week women's self-defense class (20 hours) is as follows:

Week 1

Introduction: Myths and facts regarding crimes of violence against women. Presentation of current data regarding patterns and stages of assault, victim and resister responses, etc.

Warm-ups: 15–20 minute warm-up, including stretching, strengthening, and cardiovascular exercises

Introduction of targets and weapons: Basic front-facing strikes introduced, including heel hand strike, eye gouges, eye jabs, iron hammer strike, throat jab, punch, groin grab, front snap kick to knee or shin; slow-motion continuous use of above basic

strikes, emphasizing focusing on targets (on assailant, rather than on oneself).

Week 2

Warm-up, with review of front-facing basic strikes

Introduction of front choke hold break (shin kick, flying wedge, heel hand combination)

Introduction of side snap kick to knee

Discussion of makeshift shields or weapons (an examination of common household objects that can be used as shields or weapons, such as chairs, books, cushions, shampoo bottles, etc.)

Week 3

Warm-up, with front choke hold break review

Ground defense (avoiding the fall, ground kicks, rolling breaks, body tosses, departing): This portion consists of teaching a series of skills designed to enable women to avoid being knocked to the ground. Failing that, they are taught how to prevent the assailant from pinning them. Failing that, they are taught how to dislodge an assailant and depart.

Wall releases: A defense against being pinned up against a wall

Wrist releases: Breaking one and two-handed grabs, in both assaultive and teasing situations

Week 4

Warm-ups and review of above

Introduction to the use of elbows (six different strikes, including roundhouse, hooking, back, rising, downward, and straightline elbows)

Introduction to release from rear forearm grab (elbow, back kick, scrape, stomp) and other rear approaches, including bear hugs, choke holds, wrist grabs

Shield and bag work

Week 5

Warm-ups and review of all strikes and breaks learned

Surprise attacks: People attack one another in different and unanticipated ways;

defender must think and respond quickly and appropriately.

Week 6: Confrontation training

Week 7
Warm-ups
Introduction to blocking
Introduction to evasive footwork (practice of evasive side steps in response to straightline punches and downward strikes and tenkan in response to horizontal techniques)

Week 8
Warm-ups, with review of blocking and evasive footwork
Introduction to weapons; discussion of data on assaults involving weapons
Evasive footwork applied to defense against bludgeons (using rolled-up newspapers as bludgeons and dodging them with footwork learned in previous weeks)
Immobilizing the backswing and follow-through, charging: This involves practicing techniques designed to take the defender inside the critical distance, and assumes that evasion is not possible.

Week 9
Warm-ups
Introduction to defense against a knife (discussion of active and reactive weapons: Active refers to those weapons that are in play and where immediate evasion or resistance is required to avoid being injured. Reactive refers to those weapons that are used as a substitute for physical force in discouraging resistance and forcing a woman into submission. Alternative strategies in dealing with reactive weapons are discussed.)
Practice of evasive side-step in response to downward thrust (active knife)
Use of makeshift shields or weapons in dealing with active knife or reactive knife attack (i.e., clothing, sand, coins, kicks, etc.)
Drill for dealing with reactive knives: Involves biding one's time until the risks involved in resistance are reduced, by virtue of the assailant either putting the weapon down or being momentarily distracted by something (a ringing phone, a shout, a backfiring car, etc.). While waiting for the moment of escape, people are encouraged to focus on the details of the escape: how to block or neutralize the weapon, break a hold, counterattack, which direction to run in, etc.

Week 10
Warm-ups
Defense against more than one attacker (discussing and role-playing stages of assault involving more than one assailant). In addition, the following principles are incorporated:
Avoiding the web
Determining and then moving in the direction of safety
Using confrontation techniques in order to prevent things from escalating to the point of physical violence
Once things escalate to the point of physical violence, dealing first with the person posing the greatest immediate danger
Using one's most devastating techniques; avoiding wrestling
Moving constantly
Field trip and situation analysis: Visits to about a dozen sites, both indoors and outdoors, examining different situational factors that will influence the way in which to deal with a potential attacker
Ideally, a general meeting is scheduled at the end of each term so that participants from each of the six or more self-defense classes taught can meet to socialize and also to hear speakers from local anti-violence groups, such as the rape crisis center, battered women's shelter, neighborhood watch, etc. Women are also informed about local schools for martial arts. The purpose of this meeting is to encourage participation in community anti-violence efforts.

Conditions Specific to Program

This program requires that instructors be familiar with self-defense techniques. A minimum of one year of martial arts training is highly recommended. They should be aware of the current literature on rape, battering, and sexual assault prevention. Twenty hours of class time in traditional facilities is adequate. Striking bags, mats, focus mitts, and protective equipment are optional.

Evaluation

Participants report that they gain greatly increased feelings of self-confidence, self-belief, vigilance, and competence in de-

fending themselves. To the extent that they project these feelings of confidence and strength generally, these women are much less likely to be selected as victims. In addition, one study found that women trained in self-defense are three times more likely to successfully deter assailants than are untrained women. However, it must be emphasized that this is an introductory course, providing instruction at the most basic level of skill. For those interested in more intensive and sophisticated training in this area, study of one of the martial arts is recommended.

Adventure Actualization

Submitted by: Michael Mullaney

School: Rolling Meadows High School
2901 Central Road
Rolling Meadows, IL 60008

Summary

This unit was developed for three reasons: (1) to provide a unit that was not traditional in nature and that would appeal to students; (2) to include activities that give the instructor a means for observing and evaluating the affective domain; and (3) to provide an activity in which most students have little or no knowledge or skill, so that everyone starts at the same ability level.

Outline

I. Rock climbing
   A. Explanation of equipment
   B. Safety procedures
   C. Knots
   D. Techniques
   E. Rapelling
II. Canoeing (all dry land)
   A. Equipment
      1. Different canoes
      2. Different paddles
   B. Portage
      1. One-man
      2. Two-man
   C. Safety
III. Initiative games
   A. Two-person games
   B. Small group games
   C. Full group games

Description

The teaching of the initiative games can best be explained through a few examples.
1. Trust Fall
   Equipment consists of a school desk or the end of the fourth or fifth row of the bleachers and a crash pad to put under the "trough."
   A minimum of ten students stand in pairs facing each other at arms-distance apart and shoulder to shoulder with the person next to them. Next, they kneel and extend their arms, slightly bent at the elbows, and put one arm between the arms of the person facing. All arms should be tight to each other, and each person should lean the head back. The spotter stands at the end of the "trough"

and lines up the "faller." The "faller" takes off shoes (and glasses, if wearing any) and stands with back to the "trough." Instructions are to keep perfectly straight, grab the sides of one's pants, do not push off with the legs, and do not pike the body—the faller must *trust* the catchers.

2. Poison (beam walk)

Equipment needed consists of 2 ropes per student, approximately 3 feet long, and 2 beams (2 × 4 or 4 × 4 inches) 12–14 feet long.

This game is for 6 to 14 students (or as many as beams will hold). The object is to get the students over the poison field, all at the same time and safely. The beams and ropes are at the students' disposal. This is a timed event. Five seconds are added for each time someone steps in or touches the poison field. The course can be in a straight line or can be U-shaped.

Students should be told that if they begin to fall they should let go of the ropes, so that they do not take everyone down, especially if falling back.

3. Ropes

Equipment needed consists of a 3-foot section of rope per student, and as many pairs as possible can participate. Students are instructed how to make slip knots. One student puts a slip knot of the rope over each wrist, while the other student in the pair puts one wrist in one knot, loops the other end through the partner's rope, and then puts the other wrist through the remaining knot. The students must get free without taking the rope off their wrists. Boys and girls can work together as much as possible. It is important to see that students do not get rope tangled around their necks.

4. Square Seven

Equipment needed consists of seven squares, with six participants for each group of seven squares.

Students stand on all but the middle square. The students on one-half all stand facing the students standing on the other half, who are in turn facing them. The goal is to get all the students from their original square to a square four squares straight ahead. Following the rules, a student can only move in the direction in which facing at the start. Student can only pass one person at a time and can move to any empty square only if it is directly in front. If the group gets to a position where it cannot make a legal move, it must stop, return to the original position, and start over. When a team succeeds, it should repeat the task.

5. Electric Fence

Equipment consists of two standards, a crash pad, a rope approximately 6 feet long and set 5 feet high, and a board (2 × 4 inches), beam (4 × 4 inches), or log approximately 10 feet long.

Groups of 12 to 42 members try to get everyone over the rope safely, using only themselves and the beam to do it. Any time someone touches the rope or breaks the plane under the rope, all participants must move back to the starting position (with larger groups just those touching the rope and those touching them return to the starting position). Everyone must get over safely. The group must take every precaution to insure this. Safety precautions include putting a crash pad down on the side everyone is going to. Students are not allowed to jump over the rope or to throw anyone over. Students should be in contact with someone all the way to safety. The activity must be stopped if a dangerous situation is developing. When this is corrected, the game may continue.

This unit is taught by two instructors. One instructor is responsible for the initiative games section, and the other for the skills involved in rock climbing and canoeing. The class is divided into three equal groups. When skills and initiative games are presented, one group receives game instruction and two groups receive skill instruction. They rotate the next day until each group has been at the game station once and the skill station twice. The second time a group is at the skill station, the participants aid the new group.

Conditions Specific to Program

The primary reference and the core of this unit is *Cow's Tails & Cobras*, by Karl Rohnke, published by Project Adventure, 1977. This book describes additional initiative games and some climbing skills. The initiative games provide instruction in the affective domain. Two other references were *Book of Knots*, by Clifford Ashley, Doubleday and Co., Garden City, New York, and *Ropes, Knots and Slings for Climbers*, by Walt Wheelock, La Siesta Press, Glendale, California.

Some ropes and protective equipment are necessary for the skills part of the unit. All of this equipment and some help in skills were provided by local personnel certified in climbing. Instructors are encouraged to gain skills in climbing and canoeing to strengthen the instruction. Equipment should also be accumulated. Next year, a weekend field trip to a nearby climbing area is planned for all students qualifying by receiving an A grade.

Evaluation

The unit has aroused a great deal of interest among the students. It has been evaluated as follows:
1. Written test
2. Group problem solving and oral testing
3. Observation of participation in initiative games
4. Participation in oral discussions of initiative games.

Orienteering for Secondary Students

Submitted by: Paul W. Darst
Arizona State University
Marie E. Swinford
Cactus High School

Schools: Cactus High School
6330 W. Greenway Road
Glendale, AZ 85306

Arizona State University
Dept. HPE—128 PEW
Tempe, AZ 85287

Summary

Orienteering is taught as part of a three-week unit that also focuses on backpacking and desert survival. The class meets five days a week and is open to sophomores, juniors, and seniors on an elective basis. The final activity consists of a full-day hike in the desert surrounding the nearby Superstition Mountains. Instruction takes place on the fields surrounding the school, in the gymnasium, and in the classroom. Grading depends on a combination of notebooks, written examinations, and participation in the class. This unit is one of the three of four choices that students have for this particular three weeks. Students change to a new activity every three weeks, receiving a grade in each three-week unit. The number of teachers available each period determines the number of choices each three weeks.

Outline

The following basic orienteering skills are taught:

1. Parts of the compass
2. Holding a compass
3. Directions and degrees
4. Cardinal and intercardinal points
5. Taking bearings
6. Forming a triangle and a square
7. Declination
8. Topography maps, symbols, scales, and contours
9. Map bearings
10. Pacing
11. Distances by pacing, distances by time
12. Orienteering meets: point to point, score, descriptive, and relay

The following backpacking and survival skills are taught:

1. Types of equipment—packs, tents, sleeping bags, and shoes

2. Digging a solar still
3. Pitching tents
4. Packing backpacks
5. First aid procedures

Description

Students progress through the above sequence of orienteering skills. The orienteering section culminates with a descriptive orienteering meet on the grounds of the school campus. Students work with a partner to find all ten control sites and the secret code. Each control site has a card with the bearing and distance of the next control site, as well as the secret code letter. Each pair of students is given a starting control site number and location and a meet entry blank for recording the next bearing, distance, and control cue.

Control site cards can be placed on trees, bushes, garbage cans, fences, etc. The secret code can be a series of letters, numbers, words, or names of football teams. Students can be encouraged to find the sites as quickly as possible or to take more time to be accurate with the bearings and distances. The teacher must lay out the course accurately.

Backpacking and survival skills are then discussed. The final activity is a day hike in the desert near the Superstition Mountains.

Conditions Specific to Program

Compasses and equipment were borrowed from Arizona State University, several equipment stores, and students in the classes. Other sources and references include:

1. Darst, Paul, and George Armstrong. *Outdoor Adventure Activities for School and Recreation Programs*. Minneapolis: Burgess Publishing Co., 1980.
2. Darst, Paul. "Orienteering: A Lifetime Activity for Your Curriculum." *Arizona JOHPER*, spring 1979, pp. 19–22.
3. Disley, John. *Orienteering*. Harrisburg, Pennsylvania: Stockpole Company, 1967.
4. Kjellstrom, B. *Be Expert with Map and Compass*. New York: Charles Scribner's Sons, 1975.
5. Stewart, Michael. "Descriptive Orienteering in the Elementary School." *Physical Education Newsletter*, No. 113 (March 1980).
6. Hugglestone, Arthur, and Joe Howard. "Orienteering," Chapter 13, pp. 191–200, in *Physical Education and Sport for the Secondary School Student*. AAHPERD, 1900 Association Drive, Reston, Virginia 22091.
7. Silva Company
   2466 North State Road 39
   LaPorte, Indiana 46350
8. Orienteering Services, U.S.A.
   Box 547
   LaPorte, Indiana 46350
9. American Orienteering Services
   308 W. Fillmore, Suite 105
   Colorado Springs, Colorado 80907

Evaluation

Orienteering is an exciting adventure activity that combines cross-country travel with the ability to use a map and a compass. It is similar to a walking road rally and has been called the thinking sport because rapid decisions need to be made in determining proper routes. It can be a successful activity for all ages and physical abilities. The agreeable blend of physical and mental skills can be an enjoyable experience for all ability levels.

The students at Cactus High School found this unit a reasonable alternative to the traditional team sports. Students showed a great deal of enthusiasm in terms of participation and attitudes. Orienteering also offers students exciting challenges in terms of a lifetime activity.

A detailed unit plan and more specific information are available from the authors.

Modified Orienteering as Program Enrichment

Submitted by: Dr. Don R. Andersen,
District Coordinator

School: Winnetka Public Schools
Winnetka, IL 60093

Summary

Under ideal conditions, orienteering is a sophisticated activity that calls for runners to find their way through a large outdoor area of usually rugged terrain in the shortest possible time. Critical checkpoints along the route must be visited by the runner during the run. In addition to a demonstrable ability to run long distances under difficult conditions, the runner should also possess the skills of map reading and compass use.

The dual characteristics of orienteering—physical endurance coupled with cognitive judgment—provide a challenge with built-in appeal for many secondary school students. For purposes of curriculum enrichment, orienteering takes the tedium out of distance running by adding a new dimension. The problem in using this activity in a school setting is the usual one of lack of time and space. However, it is possible to provide a form of orienteering to secondary school students during the regular physical education period by using the existing open space around the school. The answer lies in adapting the concept of orienteering to fit the particular needs of the students and to use existing facilities.

Outline

The necessary sequences for setting up modified orienteering are:

1. An area suitable for the activity and the imperatives unique to each school (class size, length of class period, etc.) must be found.
2. The area must be explored and a map made to show prominent physical features, quest areas, and the point value of these quest areas (based on distance or degree of difficulty).
3. Markers for identifying the quest areas (the places the runners will seek) and the point values must be in place before the activity begins.
4. An explanation of modified orienteering must be made to the class, describing what they are expected to do. Students are shown a large map of the

area or given individual maps. They are informed of the amount of time they are permitted to run the course and the method of scoring (e.g., individual, squad, etc.).

5. The entire class starts from a common start-finish line, and the clock begins the count-down.

6. A whistle or horn is sounded at the end of the elapsed time, and all runners still on the course are eliminated from the scoring tally.

7. The scores (based on the number and value of the quest areas visited) of those runners who returned to the start-finish line before the whistle are compiled and winners are announced.

Description

What follows illustrates how orienteering may be modified to fit a specific location. Washburne Junior High School is situated quite near a large public park. A large diagram of the park is shown to the physical education class; topographical features, buildings, and landscapes are indicated. Also shown are the common start-finish line and the point values for the various quest areas, which are specified places in the diagrammed area where the runners direct their efforts. A higher point value is accorded a quest area located farther from the start-finish line, such as a large oak tree a block away, or one that is more difficult, such as the top of a sledding hill. The point values for each area are shown on the diagram, and a cardboard number (corresponding to the point value) is placed in the quest area. The runner must actually touch this cardboard number for a score in the desired quest area.

Prior to the start, the runners are given a brief opportunity to view the course from the starting area and are told the amount of time allotted for the event. After the common start for the entire class, each runner tries to visit as many quest areas as possible before the specified time elapses. The runners keep track of their own cumulative score, using the honor system. If they fail to return to the start-finish line before the time elapses (e.g., 15 minutes), they forfeit all of their points. If they return too soon, they lose valuable time that could have been spent in visiting more quests and, therefore, earning more points.

Scoring may be on an individual basis or may be combined for team or squad scores. This activity introduces the participants to basic map-reading skills, forces them to make independent decisions as to which quest areas to visit, and fosters an awareness of their own strengths and weaknesses. It also places the student in a situation where it is necessary to react to the passage of time in a specified period, and, finally, it provides excellent practice in endurance running in an enjoyable setting. Obviously, the runner who can cover either the greatest number of quest areas, or those with the greater level of difficulty within the allotted time, wins.

In the absence of a large park area, the regular playing fields may suffice for this activity. Soccer goals or softball backstops, even electric light poles, can serve as quest areas, and they provide a convenient surface to attach the point value for that particular station. Outdoor apparatus is also useful (e.g., the top of a climbing pole or the rim of an outdoor basketball goal). Teamwork may be encouraged by making the quest on one station the cross-bar of a football goal post. As this is usually out of the reach of a secondary school student, a cooperative effort is required. Other options include the use of modified orienteering as part of field day, which is still a popular event in many junior high schools, or use of school buses to take a short field trip to a park where the necessary space to run the activity is available.

Conditions Specific to Program

The Washburne Junior High School course is kept simple, so that the students can look at the large diagram before the race and relate it to the running area. They have to remember where the higher-value quest areas are located. If the area to be utilized is particularly large or the quest areas are complicated, it is advisable to have individual maps provided for each runner. The running area should be large enough and the quests of such a challenging nature that the activity has a real meaning.

Evaluation

Strengths
1. There should be more quest areas available than any participant can visit in the specified time, thus causing the student to do some quick, critical thinking in establishing priorities. It is possible for a more alert, slower runner to achieve a higher score than a runner who relies solely on speed.
2. Modified orienteering is an activity-oriented event emphasizing endurance running without drudgery because the runners focus on the quest instead of on the exertion.
3. It is an excellent culminating activity for units on aerobics, physical fitness, distance running, etc.

Weaknesses
1. If the honor system of scoring using the hand touch is not workable, the runner should carry a small index card. When visiting a quest area, the runner makes a mark on the index card with the magic marker tied at that location. Each quest area has a marker of a different color. Points are totaled after the race.
2. The activity requires considerable pre-class preparation.
3. Modified orienteering is best accomplished in a large outdoor area. Unfortunately, such an area is not accessible to all schools. If the event is held on a smaller field, the amount of time allotted should be proportionately diminished.

General Comments

Modified orienteering is extremely successful for secondary school boys and girls. The degree of success depends on creative physical educators who can perceive the inherent value of this activity and adapt the program to fit the situation.

PART V
FITNESS-RELATED
IDEAS
Curricular
and
Teaching Concepts

Parcourse Strive

Submitted by: Al Bochman
Austin Middle School
Paul Dubois
Bridgewater State College

School: Austin Middle School
East Freetown, MA 02717

Summary

The parcourse strive program at the Austin Middle School was developed by synthesizing two existing instructional units. The parcourse or jogging/exercise trail unit was combined with our own Project Adventure program called strive. The Middle School complex is surrounded by a large wooded area which lends itself ideally to the program. The objectives of parcourse strive are: (1) to offer students an alternative to more traditional programs, (2) to attempt to direct the students' attention toward outdoor education, and (3) to promote group and individual problem solving.

The students, who are randomly grouped into squads of 6–7 participants, are consistently motivated by a series of challenging problems presented by the teacher. Once each problem has been explained, the students begin to solve it as a group or as an individual. The teacher is available to assist and encourage the groups and the individual students.

The popularity of the activity is due to such attractive features as self-pacing and self-testing activities, an aerobic fitness component, and challenging tasks requiring cooperative efforts among students possessing variable skill levels. Students also find it a great deal of fun!

Outline

I. Preliminary group lead-up situations
II. Performance objectives at each station
III. Explanation of activity within groups
IV. Carrying out of activity
V. Group evaluation
VI. Feedback

Description

The parcourse component of the unit consists of a number of exercise stations interspersed along a ¾-mile trail. The trail's introductory station has instructions for warm-up exercises, after which participants begin a short jog to station one. By jogging from one station to another and performing the varied exercises prescribed at each, participants can improve the functioning of their cardiorespiratory and musculoskeletal systems and enhance balance and agility.

The strive portion of the program offers adventure-type problem-solving activities which must be completed by the cooperative efforts of the group participating on the trail. Other stations on the trail encourage individual problem solving or provide challenging fitness activities.

The first few weeks of parcourse strive are spent preparing the students for the aerobic demands of the unit and familiarizing them with each of the station's activities. Classes sometimes begin with a series of unique warm-up and flexibility exercises taken from the Project Adventure programs. Next, the students take part in a follow-the-leader jog. The leader (the teacher, in most cases) is encouraged to make use of the entire area of fields and woods surrounding the school. A few minutes of jogging are planned for each class, and the time is gradually increased at the end of the first week. The warm-down period for each of these initial classes is spent introducing the students to the stations along the trail. By the end of the second week, most classes will have met 6 to 8 times and are prepared to tackle the trail independent of the instructor's direct guidance. The stations that have been constructed are situated so as to be within sight of a single physical education instructor.

The stations and tasks are designed to be progressive in nature. Furthermore, there are no time restraints on the tasks; the students are encouraged to work together (or individually) until they are satisfied with their level of success.

To achieve the objectives, the students must:

1. Read the problem and objective at each station.
2. Realize personal limitations in attempting to reach objectives or solve problems.
3. Work individually or within a group to accomplish tasks.
4. Pass on to the next station. If failure is met at any one station, the teacher provides feedback that can bring success at this and subsequent stations.

Example: Station 1: Tire Obstacle. A large tractor tire is suspended between two trees at a height of approximately 5 feet. Participants in each group must work cooperatively to get the entire group safely through the opening of the tire. A modification of this task would be to successfully guide as many fellow students as possible through the opening without touching the innermost circle.

Example: Station 2: Motor Efficiency Tests. This station provides a variety of self-testing activities in such psychomotor domains as balance, flexibility, agility, strength, power, and endurance. Participants may select one or several of the areas at any one time.

Conditions Specific to Program

The program was developed by a member of the school's physical education staff. Because a budgetary allotment for the program was not available, funds and materials came from several local organizations and businesses. Perhaps the biggest challenge in implementing the program was that of recruiting the volunteer help needed to construct the various stations. Scheduling of classes fell within the general constraints of other physical education programs and thus was not a concern.

Evaluation

Strengths

1. Cooperation and interaction among the students
2. Opportunity for students to learn about each others' feelings
3. Everyone treated equally, regardless of skill

4. Potential for enhancing self-image and confidence

5. Student's exposure to challenging experiences

6. Development of familiarity and identification with the natural environment

Weaknesses
1. The teacher cannot be with every group during each class.
2. Some students fail to use time wisely.
3. Some students attempt to dominate the group.
4. Lack of an adequate tool to assess cooperation within groups.

Aerobics Trail: A Special Indoor Activity

Submitted by: Jeffery J. Dorociak
G. Linda Rikard

School: Columbia College
Columbia, SC 29203

Summary

The aerobics trail aims to develop cardiovascular fitness while students engage in an enjoyable activity. The aerobics trail is useful as part of a fitness unit or as a rainy-day activity. It is appropriate for all students from junior high through college level.

The needed equipment and space include: (1) a record player, (2) several albums of rapid music, (3) approximately seven sheets of poster paper, and (4) a large space, such as a gymnasium or an empty cafeteria. From one to a hundred students could be on the aerobics trail at one time, depending on available space.

Outline

The trail itself consists of six locomotor movements: jogging, skipping, sliding, walking, leaping, and hopping. Therefore, six markers need to be constructed. Three sections of poster paper (about a foot square per section) are taped together to form a three-sided tent for each marker. On one side of the marker, in bold letters, is written the locomotor movement that is to be performed in that portion of the trail. Also, the starting point of the trail is indicated by a marker or by a chalk line on the floor.

Three markers are placed an equal distance from one another on one side of the space area, and the three other markers are placed on the opposite side. Chalked arrows on the floor make the path of the trail clear. Space is left at the end of each marker for students to move around and toward the next marker and for an outside walking lane.

Description

The trail begins at the far right corner of the open space. Students travel (or dance) through the trail in pairs. They move in straight lines following the arrows and turning at the end of each lane while changing locomotor patterns as indicated by each marker. Long lines of waiting par-

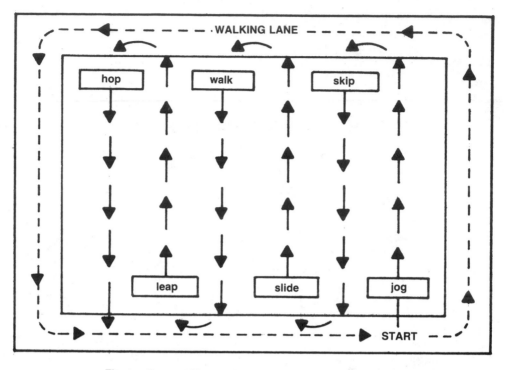

Floor pattern and locomotor movement on the aerobics trail.

ticipants can be avoided by staggering student pairs throughout the trail.

It is important to choose music with a rhythm sufficiently fast to set a pace that will elicit a training effect (70 percent to 80 percent of maximum heart rate). Beach music albums work well as pace setters. All students should be encouraged to pace themselves with the rhythm of the music, so that the entire group moves at about the same rate and so that they keep their heart rates in their training zone.

After students complete one full circuit of the trail, they should walk around the outside of the aerobics trail one time before starting again (two walking bouts, if fitness level is low). Students should continue through the trail several times (approximately 15–20 minutes total), depending on the amount of aerobic activity set by the teacher.

Evaluation

The aerobics trail has been used several times in college jogging and weight control classes at Columbia College. Students participate enthusiastically and enjoy completing the trail several times. All students maintained heart rates within six beats of their needed training heart rates, based on the formula $220 - \text{age} \times 0.75$.

General Comments

While the purpose of the aerobics trail is to produce a cardiovascular training effect in participants, modifications to the trail could focus on skill development, muscle endurance, etc. An adaptation might include tumbling movements such as rolls, dives, cartwheels, handsprings, round-offs, and other skills to be perfected by students. Combining these skills in a sequence could move the learner toward developing floor routines. Any moves or combinations of moves could be designated on markers and spaced in a manner similar to that used for the aerobics trail. Teachers need to use imagination in adapting the aerobics trail for their own purposes.

Circuit Training for Physical Fitness

Submitted by: Richard A. Eastwick

School: Haddonfield Middle School
Lincoln Avenue
Haddonfield, NJ 08033

Summary

Circuit training is an individualized program of physical fitness that includes a series of 12 exercise stations. Self-improvement is stressed, rather than competition, as students work to perform more repetitions than previously done at each station. The circuit contains exercises designed to improve many of the components of physical fitness. Overloading is achieved by performing more repetitions at each station or by increasing the time spent at each station. Students record data on personal fitness cards. If necessary, circuit training can be performed in a small space and with little or no equipment.

Outline

   I. Teacher explanation and demonstration of each exercise
  II. Student performance of each exercise at a moderate rate
 III. Student performance of each exercise for 10 seconds at a rapid rate and with adequate recovery time between exercises
 IV. Gradual increase of the time interval at each station by 5 seconds during subsequent classes until students are performing each exercise for 45 seconds.

Description

Circuit training is an individualized physical fitness program that allows each student to work at a rate commensurate with the student's level of physical fitness. During circuit training, students progress through a series of 12 exercises performed at permanently designated stations in the gymnasium. Each exercise is continued for a period of 45 seconds. On a signal from the teacher, students move or rotate to the next station. The circuit is completed when every student has performed all 12 exercises. The students are encouraged to move through the circuit, completing as many repetitions as possible at each station. Physical fitness improves as more repetitions are performed.

At the beginning of the school year, students are provided with detailed explanations and demonstrations of how to perform each exercise. The students are then given the opportunity to practice each exercise at a moderate rate. Practicing at half-speed allows the students to learn the correct mechanics of each exercise. During the next class period, students select a partner. The teacher then assigns each pair of students to a station where both perform the exercise as rapidly as possible for 10 seconds. If the class contains more than 24 students, groups of three students can be formed. The teacher times each station. The students rotate to the next station when the teacher blows a whistle.

Each class period thereafter, the time interval for all exercises is increased by 5 seconds until students are performing for 45 seconds at each station. At this point, students are encouraged to decrease the rest interval between exercises by running to the next station as quickly as possible. Periodically, students are provided with individual fitness cards to record the number of repetitions at each station. The cards are used to chart progress and are kept by the teacher in file folders.

The circuit consists of 12 exercises that place emphasis on many components of physical fitness, including muscular strength, muscular endurance, cardiovascular endurance, flexibility, speed, balance, and agility. Consideration has been given to the alternation of body parts to allow recovery. The stations generally alternate stress on the arms and legs. The circuit includes the following stations:

Station 1: Bench stepping. For muscular and cardiovascular endurance. Performed on the first row of the gymnasium bleacher seats. Bench stepping can be done on any sturdy chair or bench. The student steps up and down repeatedly.

Station 2: Sit-ups. For muscular strength and endurance. Performed on an exercise mat with the knees bent. The student clasps the hands behind the head and touches the elbows to the knee caps. For added strength, the student may hold a barbell plate.

Station 3: Alternate leg hops. For muscular power and endurance. From a starting line, the student hops across the gymnasium floor to an end line on the right leg only and returns to the starting line by hopping on the left leg only. When the starting line is reached, student turns and crosses the floor again on the right leg only, emphasizing large hops.

Station 4: Chin-ups. For muscular strength and endurance. Performed on a chinning bar. The student does repetitive chins, emphasizing complete elbow extension before starting the next chin.

Station 5: Squat jumps. For muscular power and endurance. Performed near a wall. From a full squat, the student jumps and reaches as high as possible with one hand, returns to the full squat position, and repeats.

Station 6: Push-ups. For muscular strength and endurance. Performed in a modified version on the knees, if necessary. A full range of motion for the arms and shoulders is emphasized.

Station 7: Repetitive sprints. For muscular power, speed, and agility. From a starting line, the student sprints across the gymnasium floor, stops on end line, turns sideways, and touches the line with the hand. Student then reverses direction and returns to the starting line, performing as many sprints as possible in the time period. Changing direction quickly and reaching full speed as fast as possible are emphasized.

Station 8: Horizontal ladder. For muscular endurance and flexibility. The student starts at one end of a horizontal ladder and travels the distance using the hands, runs back to the starting position, and repeats.

Station 9: Dorsal lifts. For flexibility and strength. The student lies in a prone position on a mat and lifts the head and chest as high as possible. This position can be modified by grasping the ankles with the hands. For increased strength, the student may hold a barbell plate behind the head.

Station 10: Squat thrusts. For muscular endurance. This exercise is performed on four counts, with instructions to the student to (1) squat and place the hands on the floor in front of the feet; (2) thrust the feet together, straight back to achieve a pushup position; (3) return to the squat position, with the knees tucked into the chest; (4) stand up. The student performs as many as possible in the time period.

Station 11: Rope climb. For muscular strength and endurance. The student climbs as high as possible, descends hand-under-hand, and repeats.

Station 12: Hip flexors. For muscular strength and endurance. Hip flexors can be done on a chinning bar or Universal-type hip flexor station. The student hangs from a chinning bar with the arms extended, bringing the knees up to the chest as far as possible in a tucked position and returning to the starting position with the legs straight. Vertical movement with no horizontal swinging is emphasized.

Conditions Specific to Idea

Any physical education program can include circuit training. A circuit can be constructed to fit any gymnasium, field, all-purpose room, or classroom. No special equipment is necessary.

Evaluation

Strengths

1. Circuit training can provide conditioning for an entire class of students with a wide range of fitness levels.
2. Less gifted students are not compared with highly conditioned individuals, since emphasis is on self-improvement.
3. Students enjoy the variety of activities.

4. Students welcome the opportunity to exercise with a partner of their choice.
5. Overloading can be achieved easily by increasing the repetitions, increasing the time spent at each station, decreasing the rest interval between stations, adding weight such as barbell plates to the body, or performing the circuit more than once.
6. Circuit training can be done in a small space, if necessary.
7. A circuit may use little or no equipment.
8. A circuit can stress any or all of the components of fitness and may include sports skills.
9. Student progress is readily seen on individual fitness cards.

Weaknesses

1. It is difficult to observe and encourage all students at all times.
2. Students sometimes sacrifice good form and a wide range of motion for speed during execution of an exercise.
3. A grading system is needed to provide weighted scores for highly fit individuals who cannot demonstrate increases in repetitions as can the individuals with low fitness.

General Comments

Circuit training is especially popular with middle school students because they like the variety of exercises. Since the circuit is vigorous and demanding, warm-up and flexibility exercises should be done first. For safety reasons, students must remain in a designated area for each station.

Teaching Self-Direction Through Fitness

Submitted by: Gayle MacDonald

School: Jefferson High School
   5210 N. Kerby St.
   Portland, OR 97217

Summary

Decision-making, problem-solving, and self-direction skills are essential in a democratic society. Fitness is conducive to teaching these skills. Students begin the year in a teacher-oriented setting but soon begin moving to a student-oriented focus. They are taught to set personal goals, write plans, and follow their own programs. The speed of progress is dependent on the student's readiness to take on these responsibilities.

Outline

I. Introduction to fitness concepts and activities is presented.

II. Students are given a written knowledge test and must have five consecutive "clean days" (see below).

III. Student chooses one of four teacher-written fitness contracts.

IV. Student writes own fitness contract.

V. Student writes contract that includes equal parts of fitness and skill and play work.

VI. Student writes an open contract.

Description

The physical education classes are team-taught and meet five times a week, with about 30 minutes allotted for activity time. Two days a week students participate in a wide variety of sports and activities such as volleyball, frisbee, touch rugby, relaxation, basketball, etc. One day, usually Friday, is set aside for the cooperative games and for problem-solving and risk-taking activities from the Project Adventure curriculum. The other two days students work on fitness activities and concepts, self-awareness, goal setting, and writing and performing contracts.

The first six weeks of the year are devoted to teaching traditional fitness concepts (cardiovascular endurance, muscular endurance, flexibility, etc.) and participating in fitness activities (stretching, weight training, jogging, etc.). For example, on Tuesday students would learn in a cardiovascular laboratory to take their pulse and to discover what activities give their heart a cardiovascular training effect. On Thursday they would participate in a cardiovascular activity, like easy jogging, while monitoring their pulse.

At the end of six weeks, most students understand the basic concepts well enough to begin working on their own. To prove their understanding, they must pass a written knowledge test. In addition to mastering the fitness concepts, they must show some degree of responsibility, which is measured by "clean days." A clean day is being on time, dressing (almost any type of clothing is allowed), participating in all of the day's activities, and respecting others' rights. They must have five consecutive clean days before starting on a contract.

When the requirements to begin contracting are met, the student chooses one of four teacher-written contracts (flexibility, cardiovascular endurance, muscular endurance, or general overall fitness) and follows it for six sessions. The student then progresses to a second fitness contract,

Contract No. 1: General Overall Fitness

Directions: You will do this entire contract for four days. As you do each exercise, check it off and record the amount of weight used or the number of repetitions accomplished. Except for stretching, you may do the remainder of the workout in any order. To progress to the next contract, you must pass a written fitness knowledge test.

Exercise	How Much	Dates
1. Stretching	first 5 minutes	
2. Sit-ups	20–40	
3. Push-ups	as many as you can	
4. Bench press	1 set of 15	
5. Leg curls	1 set of 15	
6. Pull-downs	1 set of 15	
7. Leg press	1 set of 15	
8. Curls	1 set of 15	
9. Leg extension	1 set of 15	
10. Jogging	7 minutes	
11.		
12.		

which is student written and is based on personal goals. The third contract is even more open, giving an opportunity to work on fitness and sport skill or play. The final contract leaves all choices up to the student for those two days a week.

Contract No. 2

Directions: Choose one or more of the following goals. Choose only goals you are sincere about working on.

1. ___ Cardiovascular endurance
2. ___ Muscular endurance
3. ___ Strength
4. ___ Flexibility
5. ___ Other _____
6. ___ Losing weight
7. ___ Gaining weight
8. ___ Toning muscles
9. ___ Relaxation
10. ___ Other _____

Using these goals, write a fitness contract that will last for 25–30 minutes.

Exercise	How Much	For Which Goal	Dates
1.			
2.			
3.			
4.			
5.			
6.			
7.			
8.			
9.			
10.			
11.			
12.			
13.			
14.			
15.			
16.			
17.			
18.			
19.			
20.			

Contract No. 3

You may now divide your time into two 15-minute segments and include a sport of your choice. In a circle, fill in the fitness activities and sport in which you wish to improve.

Examples:
Fitness: stretch 5 minutes, jog 10 minutes
Skill and Play: develop jumpshot, play basketball

I. Fitness
What? Where? Why?

II. Skill and/or Play
What? Where? Why?

Students who have not met the requirement of five consecutive clean days remain under teacher direction in "lockstep," which consists of a variety of fitness activities of the teacher's choice. In other words, choice is not given to students until they have established responsible patterns. Students in the lockstep group remain until their five clean days are re-earned, at which point they begin on the contract where they left off.

Conditions Specific to Program

Some practical suggestions follow:
1. The teacher should take attendance while students are sitting in an alphabetical circle. After roll call, on contract days the teacher reads out the list of people who have five consecutive clean days. These students stand up as their name is called and go to a certain area in the gymnasium. The instructor who is taking the con-

Contract No. 4

You may now divide your time up in any way you wish. First choose the goals you would like to work toward, then draw lines from your goals to the activities which will help you to reach your goals.

Goals

HEALTH	X Stretching exercises
Cardiovascular endurance X	X Weight training
Flexibility X	X Push-ups, sit-ups, other calisthenics
Weight control X	X Jogging
Relaxation X	X Posture exercises
SAFETY	X Relaxation
Speed X	X Self-defense
Strength X	X Karate
Self-defense X	X Wrestling
APPEARANCE	X Ping pong
Muscle bulk X	X Frisbee
Muscle shape X	X Hacky sack®
Weight control X	X Gymnastics
Posture X	X Football
ACHIEVEMENT	X Soccer
Being competitive X	X Basketball
Developing courage X	X Volleyball
Taking risks X	X Track and field
Developing talents X	X Softball or baseball
Feeling better physically X	X Tennis
PLAY	X Golf
Have fun X	X Handball or paddle ball
Be creative X	X Agility exercises
	X Balance exercises
	X Speed exercises
	X Badminton
	X
	X

tract group that day checks to be sure everyone has a contract before continuing to the area to be used.

2. If students are doing activities that are not on their contract, the teacher asks "Is that on your contract?" Usually this gets them back on task. If, after many proddings, they are unable to keep on contract, they must go back to the lockstep group for a week.

3. It is helpful to have facilities scheduled so that three days a week there is access to the gymnasium and two days there is access to fitness facilities.

4. It works best logistically for students to keep their contracts, fitness laboratory and test scores, resource materials, and self-perception activities in a notebook, which remains in the gymnasium.

5. On some days students would prefer to stay in the lockstep group, which is all right.

6. A helpful resource is *Beyond Balls and Bats,* by Don Hellison, AAHPERD Publications, 1900 Association Drive, Reston, Virginia 22091.

Evaluation

Strengths
1. Students work on their own personal goals, at their own rate.

2. Students have the opportunity to practice decision-making skills.
3. The accumulation of "clean days" provides students with immediate rewards or consequences.
4. The teacher gets to know students as individuals.

Weaknesses
1. This program looks chaotic.
2. In comparison with a more traditional program, students do not spend as much time on skill development.
3. A great deal of supervision is required.

General Comments

It is possible to teach this module alone. Two methods can be employed: (1) when students are in the lockstep group, they can be given a typed list of fitness activities which they must perform in the order listed; at the end of the period they must have their sheet initialed in order to earn a clean day. (This allows responsible students to work on their goals while at the same time providing a structure for those who are not ready to be on their own.); or (2) instead of using the lockstep concept, the teacher may have all students on contract. A student cannot progress to the next contract until six successful sessions are completed. Students' contracts are initialed at the end of each successful day.

Point Trails for Cardiovascular Fitness

Submitted by: Terry Henage
Janice Douglas

School: Mexico Junior High School
1200 West Boulevard
Mexico, MO 65265

Summary

Cardiovascular fitness is stressed as a major objective of the physical education program. One of several cardiovascular activities employed is called point trails. This progressive activity provides an opportunity for all students to better develop and maintain their cardiovascular fitness level.

A student selects one of three point trails that are marked at progressive distances. The trails are for the students to jog or run at their target pulse rate levels. Upon successful completion of the trail, the students earn the maximum point value for that trail (5, 4, or 3 points). If a student does not complete the trail in the allotted time, he still receives a minimum of 2 points for his effort.

This activity is simple to administer and can accomplish many class objectives. It is an answer to a pre-activity warm-up. It is an objective means of evaluating a student's cardiovascular fitness level and measuring a student's progress and effort. It can also be an objective method of grading student achievement. Point trails help eliminate feelings of failure because all efforts are rewarded. Students are put in a position of responsibility. They must choose the trail that best fits their needs and abilities. Point trails instill a positive attitude toward developing and maintaining a satisfactory level of cardiovascular fitness.

Outline

I. Stretching warm-ups
II. Introduction of the activity and its benefits (first class)
III. The activity itself
IV. Readings of time and recording of points
V. Cool-down period

Description

Whenever the junior high school classes are outside, the athletic field is used in developing cardiovascular fitness. Point trails is a specific activity for this purpose. First, a 3-minute period of stretching is performed to develop flexibility and prevent injuries during jogging. Then students are given the choice of three trails to jog or run for points toward their unit grade. All trails start about 25 feet apart and end at the same finish line. The students move to the starting area for the point trail they have selected. The five-point trail is 650 yards long and is to be completed in 4 minutes or less. The four-point trail is 550 yards long and must be completed in 3 minutes and 30 seconds or less. The three-point trail is 400 yards long and must be completed in 3 minutes or less. These distances are easily covered by jogging in the time required. This was calculated by marking distances, having classes jog the trails for time, and computing averages. The trails are valid for students of ages 11–15.

After students have gathered at the starting lines for each trail, a class roster is used to record the trail each student has selected. This is recorded in pencil for easy administration. If, at the end of the point trail, a student does not travel the distance in the required time, a score of 2 points is awarded next to the name on the class roster.

The students on the five-point trail start first. The instructor uses only one stopwatch. After 30 seconds, students on the four-point trail begin. In 30 more seconds, students on the three-point trail begin. Since time is an incentive, each student is told the run time on completion. Also, the instructors give praise and encouragement to students for their efforts.

After the trail run, students are reminded to continue walking and stretching for a cool-down period. The elapsed time for completion of all trail runs is approximately 8–9 minutes.

To ensure student incentives to achieve, these motivational approaches can be used:

1. Students must realize the benefits of jogging and running for fitness.
2. The instructors can ask students to keep a record of their times and measure their own improvement levels.
3. Students must be taught the importance of the pulse rate during exercise.
4. Students can be recognized in front of their classmates for making high scores or achieving outstanding scores for their ability level.
5. Students cannot be hard pressured to run at a level they cannot achieve.
6. If a student is not trying at a level of which the student is capable, the in-

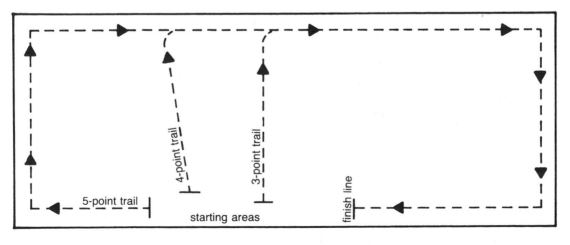

Diagram of Point Trails

structor can appeal to the student's past accomplishments and present abilities.

7. Students are reminded that the points they earn are a meaningful part of their unit grade.

Conditions Specific to Program

1. It is necessary to have an area large enough to cover the distances required.
2. The running area must be safe and runners must be visible to the instructor.
3. Directional markers can be permanent objects, like soccer goals, or removable objects, like orange rubber cones.
4. If feasible, it is helpful to chalk-line the trails for easy tracking.
5. Although this activity is easily adapted to almost any outdoor setting, it is not practical for indoor use.

Evaluation

Strengths

1. Students are put in a role of responsibility. They must earn their grade and at the same time determine their level of fitness.
2. This is a method of individualizing with students; motivational approaches are many.
3. This activity is an objective method of measuring student achievement.
4. The activity uses little time and is easy to administer.
5. Students gain social value by class interaction during the trail runs.
6. This activity can be suited for any class size.
7. The activity can be adapted to fit all grade levels.

Weaknesses

1. The activity is limited to outdoor use.
2. An area that would allow free movement for a long distance is needed.
3. Prompting is sometimes needed for some nonmotivated students; the short trail can be an easy way out for some students.
4. There is no valid way of measuring student improvement for grading.
5. Other cardiovascular activities need to be available if weather conditions cause the class to be held indoors.

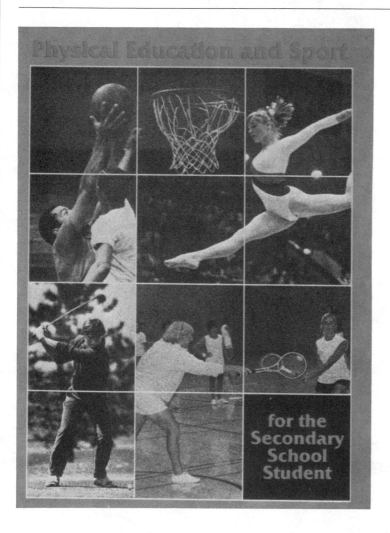

EDUCATION